pivot
with
purpose

Compiled by
Rebecca Cafiero

Published by Pitch Club Publishing

Cover Design by Jennifer Rae

Copyright © 2021 Rebecca Cafiero

ISBN: 9798525108233

To the women who are met with daily adversity yet continue to rise above: We honor you and commend you.

To all the women struggling to be seen, heard, or valued: We see you, we hear you, we value you.

Press on, continue to show up for yourself, and find your own unique, personal vision of success and happiness.

Contents

Foreword

By Rebecca Cafiero

2020 taught us countless lessons. The idea that everything we need is outside of us was illuminated as a lie, an excuse.

This time of slow living, of being inside, of having many aspects of our previous "normal lives" no longer available to us, caused us to look inward. And in that inward focus, it revealed the truth behind so many of the stories we'd told ourselves. For many, it taught us how to build our grit muscles—for others, how to find it again.

Consider: How long have you been looking for external things to fill you, to fulfill you? You've been attempting to buy or earn your happiness, but the more you consume, the emptier you feel. You've been moving so fast, trying not to miss anything. You've been doing it all but not being it all.

We've come to realize that things built on doing and having are built on weak foundations that crumble in times of challenge. This is one of those times.

In this inward place, time has slowed down enough to let us realize that everything we are seeing and experiencing is a gift, that the confusion falls away when we tune in to our own frequency, which is connected to the frequency of all that is.

This quiet time has shown us something we've been craving: more time with ourselves. We know what we need to be the lightest, brightest, most connected version of ourselves.

Now, when you look outward, the choices are clearer. Look to the noise, the darkness, the overwhelm, and you get to live there. Look to the light, to the positive, and you realize looking inward is where the calm exists.

The lessons from 2020 are many. Know where to stand your ground and where to stay flexible. Know yourself enough to not cling to something but to stand by it. Know that in different times, you need different things.

In this time, it's time to **pivot with purpose** from where you may have been heading to where you're meant to be going.

As Glinda the Good Witch famously said, "You've always had the power, my dear. You just had to learn it for yourself."

The Authors

In February of 2020, I had a deep soul calling to pause my existing business and put all of my time and effort into an idea. There was a feeling of an internal clock that was ticking loudly, and while I didn't understand it, I leaned into it.

When March hit and life as we knew it dissolved into chaos and uncertainty, with schools, parks, and all non-essential businesses closing, we headed out of the city for the still-open beach and nature. Our intended long weekend turned into three months in the small, idyllic village of Carmel-by-the-sea, a place with no streetlights, addresses, or delivery service.

I remember a moment that first weekend, just days before the world shut down, where I was overcome with anxiety and grief after a harrowing trip to the grocery store. I'd purchased the *very* last package of diapers in aisles that were empty of necessities and full of lines longer than the day before Thanksgiving. After returning to my car and peeling off gloves, I wept—for myself, for the next woman who came desperately needing diapers, for those at home without the ability to buy more, for humankind and our planet.

I knew I faced a choice that day—to continue to focus on the darkness and unknown or to pour my precious energy and focus on what I could control. To listen to the intuition that told me to carve out a place to help other women during this challenging time, pulling together my unique passions, experience, and background to create something that would have an impact much bigger than I alone could.

The eighteen women who answered the call represented different backgrounds, experiences, ages, and nationalities. Yet bound by the shared experience of choosing an imperfect time to create their dreams and doing so despite that while supporting each other as business owners, friends, and women. They grew their impacts, incomes, friendships, and most importantly, beliefs in their own unique abilities to pivot during historic times and through any challenges they meet in the future.

I couldn't be more proud or grateful for them and what the Pitch Club has become with them as the foundation.

These are the women, and these are their stories.

CHAPTER 1

Go Get 'Em, Tiger

by Elise Cruz

"If you don't like something, change it.
If you can't change it, change your attitude."

– MAYA ANGELOU

The rapidly aging basketball gym smells like tenacity, team spirit, and too many sweaty twelve-year-olds. I stand in the middle of the court, knees bent, back arched, and legs spread shoulder-width apart. I look down at my slightly parted (and notoriously clumsy) feet and wonder, "How am I going to do this?" The question bounces around my head at lightning speed as I look from my feet to the orange ball in my hands to my eager teammates. The room is packed with parents, coaches, and opponents, and every eye in the room is glued to me. I feel the seconds ticking, and I know it's time to make a decision. I have to do *something*.

Again, the thoughts start to rattle. There are so many options, decisions, and possible game plans to choose from that my so-not-a-basketball player brain is fighting the urge to melt into a puddle in the middle of the court.

Just like that, Coach Avilez must have sensed my overwhelm and started shouting, "Pivot! Tiger, Pivot!" (Yes, they called me Little Tiger on the court, not because of my athletic ability but for my fierce perseverance to get the ball, even when I had absolutely no clue what to do with it.) His words activated my training. During practices, Coach had dedicated time instructing me how to legally maneuver my body to get out of situations just like this one.

In the game of basketball, the move is called a pivot. While one foot stays firmly planted on the ground, the other foot is free to spin, rotate, and move to create an opportunity to pass the ball. It's pivoting that allows players to securely hold a firm foundation while maintaining the flexibility to change directions. Truthfully, I don't remember if we won or lost that game, but I cannot forget how pivoting allowed me to successfully pass to my teammate and, much to my own relief, get the ball out of my hands.

Thankfully for me and my *very* short-lived basketball career, the skill of pivoting extends far beyond the length of the court. Time and time again, I've relied on practicing pivoting when I didn't have all the answers but knew it was time for a change.

As a brand coach and business strategist, I've spent thousands upon thousands of hours encouraging people to take a leap, trust themselves, and make a major pivot. So why was it so difficult for me to take my own advice?

One year ago at this time, my situation looked really good on paper. I had the job, the apartment, the relationship, the car—the *stuff*. To the outside world, it all looked like everything was going according to plan, but somewhere deep in my bones, I knew it wasn't right. Day after day, I felt like I was killing myself to build someone else's dream. I put in the hours, dedicated the work, and even sacrificed my personal, professional, and interpersonal life in the pursuit of building a vision that wasn't my own. But somehow, no matter how busy or how successful, I couldn't turn off the piece of my heart that wanted more. I was sick and tired of playing behind the scenes as I watched others take the credit and glory for my hard work and big ideas. I wasn't sure how to name it exactly, but I did know that I wasn't operating out of authenticity or alignment.

I was stuck in a loop of "shoulds," "coulds," and "maybes." I felt para- lyzed, frozen in my obligations, and in desperate need of a pivot, but somehow, I never moved—until one day, I did.

What made the difference?

I had made a habit of dwelling on what was wrong, what was missing, and what I should do. It became second nature to tell myself I should change, tell myself I should be different, tell myself anything and everything I needed to hear in order to stay tethered to a situation that was no longer serving me.

Everything changed when I finally stopped talking and started listening.

It hit me unexpectedly, not in an explosive blowout, but with a moment of complete clarity and assuredness I hadn't experienced in years. I was sitting on the kitchen floor, lamenting about all the reasons I deserved more—more respect, more money, more opportunities. But as I strat- egized my argument for why I deserved a fatter paycheck, I realized no title or amount of money would ever be worth the silencing of my own voice. I realized that even if I got the exact compensation I was so desperately fighting for, it would never be enough. It could never fulfill the unrelenting sense that told me I was created for more, and it was time to pivot. Good on paper was no longer good enough for me.

I was in a job that didn't work. I was in a relationship that didn't work. I was in a community that didn't work. But it all kind of *did* work because I was forcing together all the pieces that no longer fit. I was *making* it work. In the process, however, I created space for everyone else's voice but my own. My shoulders were heavy from carrying everyone else's stuff. My back was bending under the weight of the expectation. My vision had become hazy because I hadn't practiced looking out for myself. By holding such an unshakeable grasp on who I "should" be, I was suffocating who I actually was. I couldn't shake the feeling that I was intended for more. Even though I didn't know exactly what *more* was, I knew I had to surrender the good to make way for the great.

Don't get me wrong; hindsight is 20/20 and remembering the break-ing-away process is a lot easier than navigating it, but truthfully, I wouldn't trade a moment of that painful tearing process. I had to experience the heartbreak to get to the other side. I had to let go of people I love dearly. I had to restructure and rethink my definition of success. I had to fail a lot. But most importantly, I had to remove all my protective armor, look myself dead in the eyes, and sit with the naked, raw, vulnerable version of me.

Here's what I've learned: Not all lessons are wrapped in pretty bows. Not all teachers are kind. Relationships don't necessarily end the way they began. And that's okay. It's okay that the chapter ended and the season changed. But what is absolutely not okay is making yourself smaller so others feel comfortable enough to be big.

Of course, I have gratitude for the insight, introspection, and growth those less-than-perfect situations have taught me. It took me a long time to figure it out, but I finally recognize that gratitude is not synonymous with a contract to stay. It took years of quieting my voice, ignoring my own advice, and making excuses in exchange for comfortability to finally do the brave thing and make a pivot.

When we don't listen to the calling of our innermost selves, the calling doesn't go away; it simply becomes repressed. The thing becomes like a song that's been in your head since forever: *It's a small world after all...* The song goes quiet for stretches of time, but it refuses to completely get unstuck from your head until you memorize the lyrics and sing it proudly. I've found that the smallest voice, the voice that begs to be heard and refuses to be silenced, is the very voice that *needs* to be heard. It needs to be shouted from the rooftops, shown on the big screen, and shared with the world.

When I finally made the decision to pivot, I didn't have it all figured out. I didn't have the manual with clearly labeled instructions on what to do next, which questions to ask, or who to trust. But I did have a feeling, a persistent tugging at my heart, that was growing stronger all the time.

When I left the security of my consistent job, I wasn't sure how I was going to pay my bills. When I left my affectionately codependent relationship, I wasn't sure I would ever find love again. When I took a wrecking ball to some of the major pillars of my identity, routine, community, and confidence, I wasn't sure who I would be.

I could (and in my typical high-achieving fashion, did) write a laundry list of all the things I didn't know, but I couldn't ignore what I *knew* that I knew. I couldn't unsee the once-murky realities that suddenly became crystal clear.

As I'm sure you well know, we aren't always lucky enough to have a trusted coach yelling the right answer to us from across the court, but that doesn't mean we can't pivot. I'm so grateful I finally took a page out of my own book and listened to (not just heard) my advice. It was listening to the little voice that was hoarse from screaming, "Pivot!" that led me to launch a boutique agency during a global pandemic, finally start to value my own worth, and authentically honor my core beliefs.

I've heard profound teachers and insightful thought-leaders give the advice to do *the next right thing*. Of course, I understand the sentiment, and it has anchored me through some personally turbulent times. However, if there's anything this season has taught me, it's *don't do the right thing*. It's so easy to gravitate to the right, comfortable, safe thing.

But I urge you—don't do the safe thing.

Do the thing that scares you a little. Do the thing that fires you up so much that it makes your palms sweat and your heart flutter a little faster. Do the thing that makes you feel *alive*.

Right, fine, and okay things are simply not enough. Good is not good enough. You can pivot to do the *great* thing. *You* have that strength inside of *you*.

Don't do the right thing—do the courageous thing.

Go get 'em, Tiger!

About Elise Cruz

Elise is an online business designer, builder, and integrator who provides service-based female solopreneurs with done-for-you marketing materials and sales funnels to make online sales scalable, sophisticated, and soulful. To put it simply, she's the female entrepreneurs' Digital Marketing Unicorn.

She's the full-stack digital native who is the one-of-a-kind blend of creative ingenuity, business strategy, technical know-how, marketing expertise, and passion for people.

As an ex-Madison Avenue woman turned boutique agency owner, nothing lights her up more than empowering entrepreneurs, solopreneurs, and small business owners with the tools they need to share their message in a way that actually converts and that people love. That means the quality of her clients' brands finally and unquestionably reflects the quality of work they bring to the table.

After thousands of hours spent copywriting, consulting, and brand-building, she has found one undeniable truth: An impactful and powerful brand is the harmonious intersection between your story, your business, and your ability to solve problems for your clients.

Elise on a mission to help fellow heart-led, purpose-driven female entrepreneurs unlock that magic recipe so they can stop struggling and start standing out!

www.elisecruz.com | elise@elisecruz.com | IG @elise_cruz_

CHAPTER 2

Your Great Gifts Come From Your Darkest Shadows

by Natalie Holstlaw

"Two roads diverged in a wood, and I took the one less traveled by, and that has made all the difference."

– ROBERT FROST

There's tremendous power in the Pivot. Pivot of your mindset. Pivot of your choices. Pivot of your perspective. Pivot of your direction.

Many times in life, we can only connect the dots looking backward. Oh, the complete and utter irony of the saying "hindsight is 2020" in the year 2020, a year that will go down in history as one of the most tumultuous and emotionally challenging years of our generation.

The realization hit me that everything I have ever done or experienced in my life ties directly to what I am meant to do and help people with. When the pandemic started, I observed. It's in my nature. I'm obsessed with human behavior and why people do the things they do.

I started to see a lot more anger, hatred, and violence, and a marked increase of them against women. It used to be an unwritten understanding that women, the elderly, and children were untouchable, but that ideology was shattered in front of me. During this crazy time, all of a sudden, everything that I have ever done shifted and clicked into place. Through the chaos came clarity on how I was here to serve people.

I realized that most women haven't really been taught how to create their own personal safety. There are huge gaps in understanding what they can do to keep themselves safe, and many women don't even actively participate in being an advocate for their own safety. There is still an archaic viewpoint that being a protector is only the man's role. I personally believe that women should be equipped with the knowledge, skills, and mindset to be able to best protect themselves and their loved ones.

My ability to read people and situations was developed at a young age. It was a way of emotional survival as a child, a way to sense a situation and try to anticipate things before bad things happened. It is now a gift, but it was born out of the shadows, out of growing up with a parent who drank to decompress.

My dad is the most incredible person and so involved in everything my brother and I did growing up. He taught us to hunt and fish, shoot a basketball, give people a good, firm handshake, look them in the eye, and use their name. He used alcohol to unwind, and a lot of the time, it was okay, but some of the time, it wasn't. And the challenge was that we never knew which time would be what.

I learned quickly to sense Dad's mood when he walked in the door from work, to identify if it was a walking-on-eggshells kind of evening or a playing ball outside kind of evening. Being in a constant state of emotional survival, I became highly attuned to reading people and situations and pivoting before things escalated. This emotional volatility was just a way of life. At the time, I didn't understand that I was developing one of the most important skills in my arsenal that would serve me immensely down the road in every aspect of my life.

Since I was five, becoming a police officer was all I ever wanted to be. I applied after college but was told I was ineligible for two more years because I had experimented with pot too recently. I pursued a master's degree in the interim solely because I didn't want to squander the time. My curiosity for understanding human behavior and figuring out the world beyond my upbringing was fierce, and it was reinforced when I took an opportunity to spend eight months studying and interviewing an inmate in a maximum-security prison for my thesis.

Up to this point, I was unforgiving and relentless in my thoughts around good and bad, right and wrong, black and white. I believed if you played stupid games, you won stupid prizes. I didn't expect that a man serving a life sentence would be the one to make me question my black-and-white perspective on life. My life had been a walk in the park compared to his upbringing, and yet I still struggled.

He was given up by his mother, introduced to drugs by his aunt, beaten regularly, and bounced from foster home to foster home. He was never given a fair shot at life. He was born into playing stupid games and winning the stupid prizes that went with them. Through my interviews with him, I realized he was kind, remorseful, witty, and funny—not at all the monster I was certain he would be. I couldn't look at him and his situation through my black-and-white lens anymore. It didn't fit.

I realized operating with a black-and-white perspective had made it easy for me to flippantly categorize people or situations and then write them off. I could put things in a box and make up my mind about them in an instant. Beginning to operate in the gray meant things didn't have a definitive answer or box for me to put them in, and that challenged my beliefs around certainty and what had been my truth. My incredible mother had been telling me for ages that life isn't black and white, that we must learn to live in the grey. I began to question my ability to be a good cop, now knowing that I would always want to dig deeper than face value on situations.

After I finished my master's degree in forensic psychology, the study of the criminal mind, criminal behavior, and law, I was hired on as an International Safety Consultant for an Australian company. Over the next several years, I trained over 5,000 individuals in eight different countries on five different continents. In this role, I instructed men and women all over the world in situational awareness, how our brain operates under stress, risk mitigation, engaging in challenging conversations, targeted safety training, and wellness.

Being a young female operating in a man's world of heavy construction, explosives manufacturing, mining, and so on, I was grateful for all of the hunting and fishing trips I went on when I was the only girl. Those experiences paved the way for a smoother transition into working in these traditionally masculine industries. Over the course of teaching hundreds and hundreds of hours, I had laughed, cried, delivered great training, delivered mediocre training on an off day, and been more challenged than ever by stepping into a role and leading people in learning things they didn't know they needed. And maybe even more importantly, I was learning things I didn't know I needed.

While in Pittsburgh at a client's corporate offices, my co-facilitator and I were delivering a great training in front of about twenty men, and he stepped out to make a call while I was in front of the room. I was making a long list on the full wall whiteboard as the class participants were shouting out answers. As I was writing and having to bend over to continue writing the list, one of the participants shouts out, "Hey guys, keep going—soon enough, we'll have her on her knees." In a split second, the air was sucked out of the room, and you could have heard a pin drop.

I had to make a decision about how I was going to respond to such an inappropriate comment, and I knew my reaction would determine how the remainder of the class played out. Some of these guys, in particular, the one who had made the nasty comment, were the type that if they smelled weakness, you were done. Ignoring the comment was not an option. Getting overly emotional was not an option. In a flash, I responded as coolly and calmly as I could, even though I swear everyone in the room could hear my heart pounding in my chest: "That was completely inappropriate and speaking to me that way is not okay. You have two choices: Sit there and keep your mouth shut or walk out the door. I don't care what you do either way, but if you're staying, you're staying quiet. Is that clear?"

While that situation was uncomfortable at the moment, it taught me a lot about myself, especially how far I'd come. Just a few years earlier, I had to step out of my freshman college English class for hyperventilating while trying to give a three-minute presentation about myself.

Never in a million years would I have dreamed of doing a job like this. I didn't even know it existed, and I never would've landed it if I hadn't completed a master's degree. I never would've gotten my master's if I hadn't tried pot, making me ineligible for the police department at the time I was looking to apply. I began connecting the dots looking backward.

I grew so much in that job, but I still felt unfulfilled. I had done everything I was supposed to do—go to college, get a master's, get a high-paying job—I was successful, so why wasn't I happy? I was definitely struggling with the harsh inner critic I had created for myself, moving from one accomplishment to the next but never being fully satisfied. However, I was curious that if I became a police officer, would it be the piece that would make me fulfilled? I wondered, "Am I ever going to be able to help others, create justice and safety, and improve the lives of others?"

I decided to push through my insecurities and give my dream of being a police officer another go. I was ready. I applied and sailed through the first couple of steps with ease. This is what I had been waiting for, and I wanted it so bad. And then, I failed the polygraph. I was so confused, infuriated, and soul crushed. How can you fail something when you're telling the truth? How can you get rejected before they get to know you? I felt so much shame. I was devastated because this was what I thought was my path since I was a child. Now, I was left to figure out where to go from here.

After I failed the polygraph, I relocated to a different state for my boyfriend's work. I left my big consulting job without a job to go to and found myself unemployed for the first time since I was fifteen. One month later, we found out we were expecting our first child. I lost all of the titles that had previously defined my identity; now what the hell do I do?

I could have spiraled. I thought about it. There was a part of me that wanted to because it would have been easier, easier than fighting for myself, easier to play the victim and blame people outside of myself for my failures. But because I had a child on the way and playing the victim isn't my style, I made the decision to stop the tailspin I was in. Sinking into a depression was just not an option. I had a history of looking for anything outside of myself to validate my worth, and that cycle had to stop.

Over the next eight years, I got married to an incredible, supportive man, went on to have another baby, took on my own business, and this time, I realized I had a vision for more than I was ever capable of before. I realized the stranglehold of control the perfectionist in me tried to maintain in life was just the wounded little girl in me trying to avoid feeling shame. It was a repetitive habit and my conditioned response to try to protect my heart.

This discovery paved the way for me to do something that I had avoided my whole life: be vulnerable, share my weaknesses, and talk about all the things I tried to hide about myself. When I stepped into this foreign part of me and shared my weaknesses with others, I became stronger because my self-inflicted shame was no longer strangling me. But what blew me away was how people connected with my insecurities because they related. I won a body transformation competition out of 10,000 people, represented a billion-dollar health and wellness company as their spokesperson, and spoke on stages around the country to crowds of upwards of 14,000 people about personal transformation. The work I was doing was so much bigger than me; it was about helping people visualize and take action toward a version of themselves that they thought was a pipe dream.

I laugh when I think about how I can trace all of this back to me experimenting with pot as a sophomore in college. That set off a trajectory of events that made my life grander than it would have been had things all gone according to my own personal plan. I truly believe that the universe is always conspiring in my favor, and if there's something that you so badly desire that doesn't come to fruition, it's because there is something even better waiting in the wings.

For me, becoming a police officer represented bringing security, safety, and empowerment to those that were in need. But what I see now is that

I am doing just that by combining my life experience, skills, education, and strengths and teaching women how to do that for themselves. My life goal has truly been to help other women step into being the strongest, most self-assured versions of themselves. I truly try to only speak to someone's potential as I believe a poor circumstance isn't representative of a person.

The way in which my journey toward my goal has unfolded is nothing like what I envisioned for myself; I think it's better. I stayed focused on what my heart wanted me to do, and somewhere along the way, I learned to be flexible in how I was going to get there. Now I coach women on what it looks like to create their own reality, utilize their minds in ways that get them the results that they want, and how to be a hard target when bad guys are searching for their next victim. Personal safety isn't taught to most women, and I want to change that.

Getting rejected from the police department was probably the best thing that ever happened to me, although at the time, I believed I was a failure. Rejection used to suck the wind right out of my sails. I would make my failures mean something about me as a person and less about what I needed to learn. I used to get in my own way and be so paralyzed with taking the first step because I didn't want to get something wrong.

But when you're not moving, neither is the universe. The universe waits until you make a decision and take that first step. You have to move. You have to keep going when the roadblocks and the obstacles show up. If you stop, the anxiety builds, it gains strength, and it overwhelms us, making everything seem impossible. It's like being in the middle of a meadow, with tall grass all around you and no path. You don't have to know which way to go; you just have to start. The trail will start to become clear. Now, I don't consider rejection anything but a redirection.

Have you ever stopped to look back and see how all of the puzzle pieces fit together? Have some of the most challenging moments of your life turned into being the greatest gifts you never anticipated? If that's the case, what would it be like to keep that in mind when challenges arise in the future? How would our lives be different if we defaulted to "I got this; it always makes sense looking backward."?

The quality of the questions we ask ourselves matters. Our brains are switched on by the simple act of asking questions, and they will continuously search for answers to the questions you ask. But the one thing your brain doesn't do is recognize the difference between a helpful question and an unhelpful question; it answers them just the same. One of the most powerful things you can do in your life is teaching yourself how to ask great questions! Saying, "How could I be so stupid?" versus "What can I learn from this situation?" garners a very different set of answers. One set of answers is helpful, and one isn't.

Take a few minutes to think about questions you ask yourself throughout the day. Check in with those. Is there a way you could construct them so they help your brain focus more on things that are beneficial to your wellness and your life? No matter what, if you've come across a challenge that has you stuck and the anxiety is building as you wonder what path to choose, just decide. Action negates negative emotion.

Sometimes I think we forget that we have the ability to course-correct down the line if something doesn't work out. We become so preoccupied with trying to do something perfectly right out of the gate. The most important thing is just getting started. You don't have to know the whole plan or have things all figured out. You just have to have faith that the universe has got you and is always conspiring in your favor—because it is. Take a look back at all the experiences you've had in your life and list three to five things that happened where a plot twist in your plans led you to something even better than what you were hoping for. How can you remain open to this idea and use it to help alleviate the stress in your life?

It is my hope for you, my sweet friend, that you can see yourself in my failures and my struggles so you know you aren't alone. Even more importantly, I want you to see yourself in the grit, growth, and adventure here. You are far more capable than you realize, far more intuitive than you give yourself credit for, and far more resilient than you believe. You're the type of woman who emerges from the fire stronger than before, who looks her demons in the eye and challenges them head-on.

And if you doubt yourself, know that I did, too. But one thing this great adventure has taught me is that the more we work on ourselves, the more we delve into our fears and insecurities, the more we discover and expand when we realize all of them are of our own making. If we can make them work against us, surely with a little restructuring of our minds, we can make them work for us. We are master manifesters; we will always attract what we give our energy to, good or bad, and bring into our own reality what we focus on. The key is remembering this and choosing to stay in alignment with what serves us best.

The choice is ours, my friend. Let us choose wisely.

About Natalie Holstlaw

Natalie Holstlaw is a Mindset Mentor & Awareness Strategist with a Master of Arts in forensic psychology. She is an international speaker and trainer with a background in safety consulting and psychology. Natalie has personally trained over 5,000 students in eight different countries all over the world as a leadership development coach and safety consultant. She has been featured as a keynote speaker for crowds of 12,000+ people at company events in the wellness industry. She has had the opportunity to work for Grammy-winning artists as part of their security.

Her extensive travel to over forty-five countries provides a rich knowledge to draw from with respect to human behavior and situational awareness. She had wanted to go into law enforcement ever since she was a child, but life had different plans, and she ended up marrying a federal law enforcement officer. Together, they have two children.

She is the founder of Fierce Female Collective, a community where women can come together in a safe environment to talk about daily challenges, situational awareness, and personal safety. Her twelve-week group coaching program, The Fierce Female Academy, is designed to help women smash their self-imposed glass ceilings, communicate with strength, and stand up for themselves.

Natalie's passion is to help women understand their value, create clear boundaries, and own their power so they can live safer and more fulfilled, confident lives.

www.natholstlaw.com | nat@natholstlaw.com | IG: @natholstlaw

Chapter 3

Alignment with Purpose

by Dr. Melinda Richardson

"It's okay if you fall apart sometimes.
Tacos fall apart, and we still love them."

– Dr. Melinda Richardson

Here I was in the middle of a pandemic, pouring thousands of dollars into my business, and I had to ask myself, *Is this really happening?* My dream practice arrived during the least expected time, but I jumped when the opportunity presented itself, and I surrendered to the process.

My first memory of playing doctor was at nine years old. My mother, who worked at a health center, would bring home administration carbon papers to play with. I made all my stuffed animals into my patients and went to "work" playing.

That same year, both my older sister and dad asked me to help them with their back muscle aches and pains through massages. Looking back during the stressful times with my siblings and witnessing family stress,

I was ready and willing to be the first responder to help in the only way I knew how—with my hands. The love and connection gave me a purpose. I had no idea that one day I would grow up to become a doctor of chiropractic while working with my hands.

Growing up, I had a handful of health problems. I experienced excruciating earaches, a sensitive stomach, and allergies. I had a few physical traumas, too: a fall from my bike, a go-cart crash, and sports-related injuries. Our family only went to a medical doctor for our injuries or health concerns, never considering holistic health care providers like an acupuncturist or functional medicine doctor.

In my late teens, more than a decade of softball caught up with my body. I played softball from the age of five through high school and participated in year-round leagues. I was on two first-place teams, had pitched shutout games, and was named the MVP of our division. It was hard work, and I loved it. After twelve years of softball, my shoulder felt like there was an ice pick lodged in my neck. The pain was sharp and unbearable. I was forced to abandon the sport I loved.

My unresolved pain may have cost me a scholarship to college, and just as importantly, placed a financial burden on my family. We, as a family, had invested so much in me playing softball. I had to give up on my future in softball. That was a hard pill to swallow. Had I known what I know now about chiropractic today, I may have continued playing.

I became a certified massage therapist my first year out of high school, marking the start of my health and wellness education. My dad was seeing a chiropractor at the time and encouraged me to come and watch his adjustment to see if it was something I might want to do. I sat there and watched my dad lay on his side and get his lower back adjusted, and it made a loud sound, followed by a relaxing sigh. My jaw dropped, and I couldn't think of anything more amazing than the skill and the art I had just witnessed.

I was instantly drawn to chiropractic, to helping people feel relief naturally, to helping them move better, with a gentle push called an adjustment. After undergrad, I went to learn more about the science, philosophy, and art of chiropractic at Life Chiropractic College West in Hayward, California. When I finished chiropractic college, the most challenging part of my profession was about to begin—starting my own business, becoming an entrepreneur, and soon after, juggling being a mom.

Five years after graduating, I married my best friend, Rob, and became a mom to our beautiful daughter, Sirena. Our daughter was born at home during a planned home birth. I was blessed to be a stay-at-home mom and work my home-based nutritional business part time and online. While I was grateful to work from home with my daughter, it had its challenges.

Holding my daughter on one hip, multi-tasking, lifting her to and from the crib and bathtub, and picking her up from the floor every day wore out my lower back. Once I restarted the physical work of a chiropractor in the flexed forward position, adjusting patients on a low table, my back began failing, and I needed to see several health professionals. Ironically, these are the types of injuries I see in my patients every day.

My back pain was so bad I had to see my massage therapist, an acupuncturist, and I even went to see my colleague for chiropractic. We compared a current X-ray to my first X-ray from chiropractic college, and my posture appeared to be getting worse. I thought, how is this possible? I've been getting chiropractic care for ten years.

My organs were not flowing the way my body was designed, and I knew it all stemmed from the low back pain that had been accumulating. I hit rock bottom when I got pregnant again, but sadly it was an ectopic pregnancy, and the baby did not make it. I ended up in urgent care from the excruciating pain that I felt from the baby being lodged in my fallopian tube.

My body was failing me, and it was difficult to do my job. I worried about how I'd be able to help people through chiropractic. I had invested so much of my time, effort, and money into becoming a doctor, and now, I wasn't certain I could help people with their health concerns when my own health was giving up on me.

"You don't have to see the whole staircase. Just take the first step." – MLK

Getting this far as the first female in my family to receive a doctorate degree in a four-to-one male-dominated profession has been a major accomplishment of my life! I am blessed because my family has been supportive of my dreams of helping others. In my fourteenth year of private practice, I cannot describe how much I enjoy my profession as a doctor of chiropractic. Choosing this path is one of the best decisions I have ever made.

Last year, 2020, was a challenging and interesting year with many curve balls thrown my way. I had wall-kicking moments, and it was overwhelming at times. The reality was I had to slow down as everything shut down in order to speed up the vision I have held close to my heart for several years.

My softball mindset carried over to my current attitude and approach to life and business. Keep playing the game and don't quit. Quitting is the only way to lose, and I want to win at everything I do. The pandemic forced me to move through all my challenges with a winning attitude, because in my mind, there's absolutely no other option.

When people assume you've been an overnight success, they don't realize the history of dreams and hard work. In 2011, I was a stay-at-home mom working online. I came across an online video of my friend's chiropractic practice, and I caught the vision of what I wanted my dream practice to look like. The layout of her office was beautiful, the equipment was interesting, it was something that I had never considered. I knew I really wanted to look more into practicing similar to this.

This vision of my dream practice stayed alive on my vision board. I cut out the photos from the catalog of the equipment I wanted, posted a photo of the X-ray room design and machine, and wrote down how much they would cost. I posted the certification course and photos of the actual facility I would be learning at. Even the possibility of writing a book was planted in my heart a few years ago. When you have a vision, make it happen ahead of time by cutting out the exact images of what you want.

In February 2020, I dyed my hair red in the spirit of the Niners and my girl's trip to Miami for Super Bowl LIV. While I was getting my hair done and chatting with my hairdresser, the topic of remodeling my office came up. I told him how I really wanted to open up the space for new equipment and install an X-ray unit. In addition to being a stylist, he's a handyman as well and offered to help me take on this dream project of mine. He told me he'd come by and take a look at my facility and give me some ideas on how to expand.

I felt hesitant because I didn't know how it could all work. I had already talked to a handful of contractors and received several estimates that were well beyond my budget comfort levels. He and I must have come up with about half a dozen combinations for the layout of my office.

During the early pandemic, in the months of March, April, May, and June, my office stayed open as an essential business, though we experienced a significant drop in patient flow. I experienced the same fear of the virus we all did and the uncertainty of my business surviving.

Every night, I prayed with my family. We prayed for everyone with COVID-19 or affected by the pandemic. We prayed that people trust in their bodies to heal if they ever get exposed, for them to be immune strong, and we prayed that their fears through these uncertain circumstances ease.

Then July came, and COVID made its rounds at the practice and my inner circle. My business stopped, and life came to a complete standstill. There were feelings I have never experienced before in practice. Hopelessness was one of them. It took a few days and many discussions with my close family and friends about what was going on and what could be done about it. It was one of those moments in life where you either give up or dig deep and keep going. I decided to keep going!

I called up my hairdresser and initiated Project Expansion at the office. There were financial obligations to make this happen, and the income flow was currently at a halt. Small business loans were available, and the rates were better than I had ever seen. Taking on more risk and more debt is never calming, but looking at everything that happened and what was going on, it was the perfect opportunity to do that remodel. I applied for the loan, things were getting started, and the entire project was making headway.

We slowly opened in August, with one side of my practice consisting of flooring and a chiropractic table, and the other had open walls, no floors, and construction chaos. We took action anyway and helped the people we could who needed our help. We had to be flexible, adapt to the environment, and adapt to patients' comfort levels around the construction and the pandemic. I took messy action against all odds because the only way to level up is by moving through it. You have to move through the fear, the judgments, the rejections, and the things that won't get you to your dream vision.

Weeks later, our family house in the foothills of San Jose was evacuated right where the wildfires were raging close to our home. I remember the night we had to pack our bags, thinking this could be the last time I'll see our belongings and house. We ended up sleeping in a hotel for a few days, full of anxiety and uncertainty. This was yet another experience with the hopeless feeling. Fortunately, the fires calmed down, and the winds were in favor because our home was safe.

I kept asking myself, "What's next?" The practice was still closed—we had no revenue coming in, new debt, and we just barely made it through the California wildfires. I had to surrender to the process for one more shutdown during the X-ray installation for a week.

Early in 2020, I had committed to learning more, and I was not going to let the pandemic change that. I just didn't expect the education to be timed during a COVID and fire shutdown. During that time, I took a six-module course for an intensive week-long training in the basic certification for the technique I practice called chiropractic biophysics. As a result, I'm adding more value to my patients, and the results are showing up faster. It has been a wonderful investment.

A doctor friend presenting the course reminded us that money is available to afford our equipment, to not tell ourselves the story that we can't afford it because we just might be able to if we tried to apply. I stopped making excuses and decided to go for it. And looking back, it's beautiful when you can see the "how" unraveling and conspiring to make your vision a reality. The seeds I planted several years ago were taking real-life shape and form, and now, it was all happening so fast.

While researching loan relief, I stumbled upon a gem called LoanGifting. com, similar to a GoFundMe account but for your loans. You can open up your platform similar to a Facebook profile and upload your story and also a video. Family members and friends can give you what you need versus what they think you want for holiday gifts and birthday presents. So far today, I've received more than $3,000 in loan gifts.

And now.

The practice has re-opened with the beautiful remodel expansion, and things are improving beyond my wildest expectations. I even have other career opportunities opening up after all of this, something I wouldn't have imagined in a million years. Looking back at those hard and challenging times in 2020, the ones where all hope was lost and giving up felt like the best option; those were the times where growth happened—the magic moments. They seemed so horrible at the time, but looking back, I'm thankful for them. I've found that life has rewarded me over and over again. When I don't quit, the blessings and rewards show up.

I wanted to expand and remodel before COVID. I was planning on it but didn't know how to get the remodel done and not interrupt the practice. I could not have imagined closing my doors to renovate and deny my patients their care needs pre-COVID. I thought to myself, *How on earth will I pull off shutting down to renovate?* It was scary to take this leap of faith, both emotionally and financially.

It does not hurt to shop around or test drive prior to making those big leaps of faith. Initiate the process even if it is not perfect timing or you do not think you're ready to say yes to it today, tomorrow, or next month. All these actions were imperfect actions, but I took those actions anyway because eventually, I got it right.

I shut down a total of seven weeks during COVID. I stayed the course and committed to the outcome. I accomplished so much in so little time. I experienced my most successful month, I've had a record-breaking week, and I've completed the first phase of my dream practice—all during a pandemic. And I am co-authoring this book! I can't help but sing that Arianna Grande song, "I want it, I got it, I want it, I got it." Remodel? I got it. X-ray installed? I got it. Home is safe? I got it. Certified in basic chiropractic biophysics? I got it.

Mentoring new young professionals to learn faster from me and to borrow my belief? I want it. Prior to COVID, I had offered one amazing feature in my practice: the adjustment. Now, I added value through adjustments and CBP traction, X-rays in the facility, and virtual education for patients. Next is coaching new doctors.

The challenges in between where I was nine years ago to where I am now all have one common denominator: They were all based on acts of faith. That feeling of surrender, letting go, and letting God take over was my secret sauce that carried me through it all. I've heard several times in my self-development wisdom messages that the "how" is none of our business. All you need to remember is why you want what you want and stick to the vision! In hindsight, it's a miracle that I can sit here today to tell you I've accomplished the seed that was planted several years ago and kept it close to my heart until it became a reality.

"We never know how far something we may think, say, or do today will affect the lives of millions tomorrow." – B.J. Palmer

About Dr. Melinda Richardson

Dr. Melinda Richardson is a doctor of chiropractic, basic certified in chiropractic biophysics, and owner of The Posture Lounge in San Jose, California, a chiropractic posture corrective facility that uses advanced imaging and tailored posture solutions.

After years of adjusting patients, she was frustrated to discover her patients' posture and alignment were not improving with adjustments alone. In fact, her patients were not the only ones not getting the best results—Dr. Melinda's health was declining from her own poor posture. She knew there had to be something more that could get herself and her patients the life-changing results to improve the way the body flowed and functioned.

Dr. Melinda has a passion for facilitating her patients and educating the community on the link between posture and overall bodily function. She utilizes her personally developed S.P.I.N.E. process to help people become aware of their posture and use a natural approach for creating sustainable lifestyle habits.

www.posturelounge.com | DrMelinda.Richardson@gmail.com | IG: @theposturelounge

Chapter 4

Following a Feeling

by Marlys Yvonne

"Start small, follow your breath."

– Unknown

Six months after moving to San Francisco to join a dance company, my partner dropped me during rehearsal. I shrugged it off and kept dancing. Over the next four months, the pain became worse and worse. Mornings were the hardest. I would rock myself back and forth until I was able to sit up on my bed. The pain of the effort took my breath away. I took four ibuprofen with breakfast and another four before company class. One day I couldn't get out of bed at all. I got an X-ray and learned I had been dancing with a fractured rib.

I was out for the rest of the season. Every day I went into the studio to watch rehearsal on the sidelines. I didn't dance again until the next year. At the end of that season, my contract wasn't renewed, and none of my auditions for other companies panned out. Rather than try to make it as a freelance dancer in one of the most expensive cities in the country, I moved home to Baltimore. I was twenty-two and leaving the career I had dedicated myself to since childhood.

Seven years later, I run my own business, Ara Pilates + Movement, offering Pilates-based fitness classes in the Coachella Valley of southern California. You might think my story is one about seizing the opportunity of my injury to make a decisive, deliberate change in my life, or that I had a vision for creating my own boutique studio, and my injury was the unexpected push I needed to actualize my dream.

But that is not my story. When I look back on that time in my life from the perspective of where I am today, I don't see leaving dance as the point in which I made a decisive life pivot. When I try to understand how I got to where I am, I see that all my most impactful changes weren't big, drastic movements at all but small, gradual shifts.

The idea of a quick and complete life transformation is alluring. In America, we emphasize the stories of those who take risks and make big changes: entrepreneurs who drop out of college to start the next billion-dollar company, celebrities who lose a hundred pounds of weight, underdog athletes who push themselves beyond the endurance of their more favored rivals. These become our examples of how we should change—suddenly and drastically. Like many mass media messages, this one is misleading because it makes us feel like our everyday decisions don't add up to anything.

The truth is that the majority of our lives are composed of the ordinary. Even in a pandemic, we wake up, eat breakfast, brush our teeth, buy groceries, be patient in traffic, and try to care for the people we love in the ways they need. You can always take advantage of the extraordinary, but how do we discover change when the ordinary is all we have?

The answer is to focus on the small changes that can accumulate, over time and with consistency, into an equally major shift.

That was a lesson I had yet to learn when I returned home to Baltimore. I felt defeated, wondering and not knowing what would come next. I was tired all the time. Leaving professional dance felt like losing seven years of my life, my dreams, and all the hard work I had put into it. It was my identity. I had gotten great at muscling through the hard work, the pain, the sacrifice, and the loneliness.

Long ago, when I first started to dance, the dream of dancing with a professional company inspired me to do my best. I truly and deeply loved dancing. I still do. But over time, my need to prove myself to people—prove that I belonged there, prove that I was the toughest, hardest-working dancer in the room—grew greater than the love I had for dance itself.

In my heart, I was already gone, even while my body stayed behind to go through the motions. My physical injury mirrored my spiritual journey, and I could no longer ignore the wrongness of it all. Yes, I was ready to start over, but start over as who? To do what? For years, I had tried to use big change as a catalyst to chase down a sense of happiness. I had moved seven times in seven years, using each move, each new apartment, as a forced way to restart. With each new move, I thought that this time would be the time I would find what I needed for it to feel right. I would find my coffee shop, a charming local spot, somewhere I could feel at home. The joy of unpacking my things in a new space and starting fresh allowed me to believe that this time, it might feel better. It never did.

Moving home broke the pattern, but I still didn't have a direction. I taught a lunchtime Pilates class at the John Hopkins University gym. I worked on small, experimental dance projects with a few other young drifters.

Eventually, I reached out to an old friend—another dancer with a similar story to mine. She, too, left home early to pursue a dream of dancing but had shifted course to choreographing, filming, and directing in Seattle. She knew the toxicity of the dance world and was in the process of unraveling from it without leaving it behind. She was listening to herself in a way that was leading her forward on her unique path.

Where would it take me if I listened to the voice of my own feelings? What would happen if I slowed down and listened like she did? I started to wonder what my life would have been like if I hadn't taken eight ibuprofen a day to push through the pain. What would happen if I just let myself feel rather than tell myself what I was supposed to feel? What if giving in wasn't giving up?

That summer, I bought a car and drove to Seattle. I didn't know if it would work, and that was okay. I had left behind the idea that every day had to be a performance. Each day I tried to do what felt right in my heart. I started to listen to myself. And things started to click.

I got my full Pilates instructor certification. I started teaching group classes, then private lessons. People responded to me in a way I had never experienced before. My instruction offered a nourishing alternative to the no-pain, no-gain fitness mindset that had led so many of my clients down paths of injury and discomfort. They felt better in their bodies after a class with me. Eventually, opening my own studio simply felt like the next practical step. I had no idea it would lead me to southern California. At the time, all I knew was that I had walls to paint, machines to buy, and clients who wanted to feel freedom from useless pain—a freedom that I had only just learned to give myself.

When I danced professionally, I had never let myself wonder or feel what it means to find ease, to feel something that just clicks. I've learned that you can't force what isn't meant to be, in body or in soul. Now, I feel for the difference in my effort; I feel for the ease rather than the proof of pain. The Ara practice is about letting go of externalized fitness goals and finding more space for movement in our daily lives. It also means finding more pleasure and ease in everything you do. I tell my clients what I tell myself: What feels good in your body is what's good for your body. Start small. Ignore the mirrors. Follow your breath.

The practice of Pilates is the practice of these small changes. It is the quiet decision to try and do everything just a little bit better, a little bit more fully, more precisely, every time you come into the studio. Small but consistent actions will grow into a fulfilling, stable alternative to the cyclical disappointments that come from trying over and over to force large changes quickly. Through the practice of small changes, you will not only feel better, but you will also become better at noticing how you feel. This is the deepest and most enduring gift of all.

The strength I used to feel by pushing through has been replaced by the strength I achieve when I listen to my instincts. If I hadn't learned to listen to myself, I wouldn't have been able to recognize the small steps that were right in front of me. As I lead Ara into a new year, I am guided by my conviction that our most transformative life changes are the ones we make gradually and with graceful determination.

About Marlys Yvonne

Marlys Yvonne is a Pilates instructor, studio owner, artist, and creator of the Ara Movement and practice. Her training as a classical ballet dancer helped mold the Ara practice, which focuses on thoughtful transitions, mind-focused movement, and an educated, contemporary approach to teaching Pilates.

Marlys completed her Pilates certification through Vitality Pilates in Seattle and completed further education in San Francisco, New York, San Diego, and Baltimore. She has used her unique method to cross-train NFL players, pre-Olympic swimmers, professional ballet dancers, and elite tennis pros.

Marlys works with clients of all levels, ages, and abilities to experience a deeper understanding of their bodies, create a lifetime habit of exercise and movement, and simply feel good. The Ara practice is about letting go of externalized fitness goals and finding more space for movement in our daily lives.

www.arapilates.com | info@arapilates.co | IG: @thearamovement

CHAPTER 5

Redefining Your Success & Bliss

by Gabriela Toro

*"Following all the rules leaves a completed checklist,
following your heart achieves a completed YOU."*

– RAY A DAVIS

I've always found it fascinating how the quality of our thoughts creates our physical reality. What we think becomes what we feel, which dictates our behaviors and actions, leading to the reality that we are currently experiencing. The meaning behind this changed my life.

We all make daily decisions to think positively or negatively. Whatever direction we take, it is just that—a choice.

Unconsciously or consciously, we make decisions like choosing the clothes we wear, the food we eat, the people we surround ourselves with, the information we consume, and even what we believe in.

The feeling those choices give us will create the reality we experience.

My name is Gabriela Toro, and I am an online career coach and full-time digital nomad. I went from being an overworked and underpaid veterinary technician living paycheck to paycheck and drowning in student loan debt to a six-figure online business owner and mentor to thousands while traveling the world full time. This transition happened in less than two years. Stay with me, and I will share with you exactly how I made that happen and how much the quality of my thoughts influenced this shift.

So let's go back.

I grew up in Venezuela, a beautiful country in South America. In 2011, at age eighteen, I moved to the States, escaping the dictatorship my country was suffering from.

In a day, I found myself adapting to a new culture, schedule, community, environment, and overall lifestyle. It was a transition that initiated a forced yet necessary change—to understand and grow into the person I was destined to become.

A lot of us found ourselves in this awakening phase during the pandemic. The curfews, quarantine restrictions, canceled events, and travel restrictions stripped us away from all superficial and physical reality in our routines, relationships, jobs, and activities.

These changes didn't create problems but enhanced what was already there: the deep-rooted limiting thoughts, unstable relationships, negative emotions, and unaligned tasks.

When enhanced, it made us look inward and witness a *massive* reality check.

Well, my reality check came three years earlier than the pandemic. In 2017, I intentionally took steps to become the architect of my reality, leaving a "good enough" life for a great one!

It was a rainy day in California, and I had to commute over an hour to work. I was a veterinary technician at the time, and my schedule consisted of going into the clinic before sunrise and leaving after sunset.

I sat on my bed for a minute and started thinking about what my day was going to look like, counting the hours I was going to spend in the car and at work. It equaled fifteen—fifteen hours driving and doing a job that felt hypocritical to me, promoting and practicing Western medicine when I was personally thriving and embodying Eastern and holistic practices. I caught myself showing up without feeling motivated or called to, settling for a paycheck that made me feel undervalued.

I was twenty-three, exhausted, unmotivated, underpaid, and unhappy. That day, I decided I was *not* spending those fifteen hours feeling that way ever again.

In one short year, I earned my health coaching certification, graduated with six paying clients, quit my veterinary technician job, picked up dancing again, lost ten pounds, gained mental clarity, and reintroduced happiness into my life. I called this year *the blissful step*, which became my brand and mission.

My mission is to teach purpose-driven humans how to step into the fearful and uncomfortable journey of letting go of what doesn't serve them to finally live intentionally. But how? The question we ask ourselves as soon as we start dreaming. How do we let go of all the baggage that keeps us from living the reality we truly dream of?

The answer is simple—not easy, but simple, as is life.

After intentionally and carefully reviewing my own transformation and the journey of the 100+ entrepreneurs I've helped, I can definitely say that the answer to starting a happier and successful journey is adopting a solution-based mindset influenced by your *own* definition of success.

And this is where we go back to the quality of our thoughts.

We can't even begin to think about living our wildest dreams without changing and reprogramming our thoughts, behaviors, and actions.

So let's dissect this a little further.

Success is a feeling all humans crave, give meaning to, and work toward. However, as we start understanding and working toward this feeling, we unintentionally overcomplicate the simplicity of defining it.

Humanity unconsciously confuses the true meaning behind having a successful and well-rounded life due to our current fast-paced, social media-focused, and technology-dependent world. It becomes easy to associate success with money, fame, and looks.

Let's understand a very common example to bring context to this idea.

Liz is a twenty-three-year-old college graduate who just completed her psychology degree. After desperately looking for a job to start paying her student loans, she starts waitressing at a local pub. However, she promises herself that this is just a bridge job and that what she truly wants is to help people with healthy mindset habits.

Every night she lays in bed scrolling on Instagram, Tik Tok, and YouTube to watch young entrepreneurs share their best tips about healthy habits. She studies and consumes their content blindly and consistently. This goes on for six months, which then turns into a year—a year of comparison, disappointment, fear, and obstacles, a year that lacked clarity, support, and drive.

Liz is not lazy or unmotivated. She wakes up every day and works hard, pays her student loans, and is a sweet girl trying to be happy.

So what is Liz missing? Why is she still stuck at that job?

Simple: the quality of her thoughts.

We can't initiate change and embrace our journey to success without reprogramming our thoughts, behaviors, and actions.

Where is Liz consuming information and getting clarity and support? Social media.

Since the onset of the COVID-19 pandemic, we've spent an increasing amount of time using technology as means to connect, entertain, and work. After making this our new norm, the reliance on social media is a rewarding distraction and fogging our true meaning of life.

Without a true meaning and defined concept of success, there is greater space for confusion, comparison, fear, uncertainty, and unhappiness.

That's the question I asked myself that day, sitting on my bed and reflecting on my fifteen-hour-long workday ahead—the very question I would ask Liz.

Why am I doing this? What am I working toward? What is success to me?

A huge percentage of us live our lives on autopilot. No one really knows why they have the job they have, live the way they live, and buy the things they buy. We just go with the norm, what's "in," and the best trend to keep us in the "wanted" status, drifting us further away from our own essence, feelings, and definition of happiness. As a consequence, dressing up success in the wrong costume leads us to an unfulfilled life.

So there is Liz, and there was me, working just to pay loans, waking up just to fulfill someone else's schedule and dreams with no guidance, clarity, or intention.

Do you see the gap? The pattern? Do you see why our poorly influenced and unintentional thoughts can have a drastic influence on our emotions and the reality we experience?

That is the gap I've dedicated my life to fill—to make this world a better home for all of us. After working in the online space for four years and realizing how much technology affects our thoughts and daily choices, I shifted my career to become an online business mentor, to help guide, motivate, and equip people like Liz—aspiring entrepreneurs—to intentionally define and prioritize their bliss by building a freedom-based lifestyle leveraging the online platform, but also adopting digital wellness into their routine.

As I continue working with digital hobbyists all over the globe, I continue perfecting the ultimate secret sauce to success and bliss.

I'll leave you with the following thoughts to help you simplify your life and enjoy your professional and personal journey to success.

- What is success to you? Redefine this every month. Always keep in mind: This personal vision is only defined by *you* and only you.

- Let your days be driven by your inner work—self-development, positive and solution-based thoughts, good energy, and spirituality.

- Normalize a solution-based mindset. Focus on what you have rather than complaining about what you don't.

- Practice digital minimalism and set your own boundaries. Dive into the new field of digital wellness.

- Never underestimate the power of simplicity and nature. Go back to basics.

- Use technology as a tool, just like you would a chair.

- Most importantly, live intentionally happy.

However you decide to take action, you are right.

Whatever you decide to think, you will experience.

Whatever you decide to accept, you deserve.

However you decide to live, it is just that—a choice.

About Gabriela Toro

Gabriela is a bilingual accredited career coach, full-time digital nomad, and certified digital wellness educator. She's passionate about helping new digital entrepreneurs build an aligned yet profitable business foundation so they can reach their *personal version of success*. Before becoming a business mentor, her background as a certified health coach and fitness instructor helped her study the online coaching and service-based industry thoroughly to craft her methodology for taking ideas 100% online.

Now, she teaches the same strategies that she used to build, launch, and scale her online business to help others do the same. With more than four years of online experience, she has helped hundreds of aspiring entrepreneurs from all over the globe transform their passions into full-time profitable online careers through her signature nine-day Jumpstart Your Business course.

She loves seeing her students and clients get the strategies they need to launch their own digital offers while always prioritizing their own mental and physical wellness by incorporating digital minimalism.

www.theblissfulstep.com | gabby@theblissfulstep.com | IG: @theblissfulstep

CHAPTER 6

Stop Me If You Think You've Heard This One Before

by Natalie Boese

"There is a crack in everything. That's how the light gets in."

– LEONARD COHEN

"God, grant me the serenity to accept the things I cannot change, the courage to change the things I can, and wisdom to know the difference."

Just like my computer's operating system, the serenity prayer has been running in the background of my life, allowing the applications to run smoothly and my life's choices to turn out well.

What can I change, what do I need to change, and what is perfect exactly as it is?

◆

The tennis courts were eerily quiet for a Saturday morning. Not many members had come to the club, but we had the semifinals left to play. It was the first time I had to sign upon entry to prove I was in good health, and it was the last time I would slide through the clay to return a fore-hand with a satisfying *thwack*.

It was March 14, 2020, and this would be my final social event before the world turned on its axis. My eldest son Owen was on vacation in Costa Rica with my ex-husband, and my youngest son Rhys was in the respite home for March break. This was my time for *me* to fill my cup and try to exercise, clear my head, and finally complete the things I felt like I never had time for. It was the time I needed to catch up on, well, my life.

My tennis partner and I won the match and had celebratory drinks after-ward with our opponents. We talked about how weird this felt, and it was hard to think about anything else. I kept it light, but I had this creepy feeling like there was going to be a zombie apocalypse. Who did I want on my team, and what are their super skills that are perfect for when the world was about to end? Sigh. Yes, these are the things I think about in my spare time, and yes, I am a full-grown adult.

I went home and tried to enjoy my time alone, but there was a barrage of news articles warning us of how many hours it would be before the Canadian borders would close. It was such a bizarre time, like a bad dream. I had no control over when my son's father would bring Owen home, and I had no idea whether he was truly safe. All I could do was put my faith in his dad that he was making the right decision and wait.

It was out of my hands. It felt out of control, and somehow... I had been here before.

◆

I spent the next seven days waiting for Owen to return to Toronto. I moved from one room to the next, berating myself for not using my free time better and for being worried when I knew I shouldn't over-react. Once my two small fries were home and in isolation with me, I felt complete again.

While I started to reset my gears, I saw those around me start to deteriorate—panicked conversation on the street, stockpiling of groceries and cleaning supplies, and bare shelves in the grocery stores resembling stories my mother told me about her life in Estonia as communism and war overtook her country. As long as I stayed away from what used to be normal, I was fine. In fact, I was starting to thrive.

Never managing to take the easy route seems to be the unwavering story of my life. I spent years of infertility watching my friends get engaged, married, pregnant, and have multiple children in the time it took me to conceive just one. When I finally succeeded in having two boys via in vitro fertilization, it was such a gift. The night before my second and youngest child Rhys was born, a friend asked me whether I wanted a boy or a girl. I told her, "It doesn't matter to me at all as long as our baby is healthy." Sometimes I think the universe likes to give me a challenge to see how I can adapt and grow stronger, and it just knew I was meant to be the mother of such a sweet spirit.

Rhys was born during a planned C-section. He was absolutely perfect with a little shock of brown hair and deep brown eyes. We were blissfully happy, tired, and excited to share this new being with his older brother Owen. Then Rhys turned pink and squirmed. Since this was my second baby, I wasn't initially alarmed, nor were the nurses. I wasn't worried until he stiffened and tightened up his face repeatedly. It took multiple calls to doctors and nurses before they personally saw it happen and instantly hooked him up to monitors. As they wheeled him into the NICU, I felt in my heart of hearts that it was going to be okay. What kind of okay it was going to be, I didn't know.

Growing up, I was the type of girl who always had her pencil crayons sharpened, all facing the same way perfectly in the pencil case. My drawings were always within the lines, and I followed the rules as best I could. As I grew, I created labels and systems to shelve my bed sheets and household supplies. Unknowingly, I had a desire to control my immediate surroundings that carry on in my life to this day.

And sometimes, you have to let go of the control.

I will never forget lying in my hospital bed seeing the nurse roll the empty bassinet back into my room without Rhys. My baby wasn't here. It wasn't okay. Hours turned into days, and weeks turned into seasons. Supportive friends came to visit us at SickKids, the world-renowned hospital for sick children in Toronto, and I still had so much hope that we would overcome whatever was wrong with Rhys. When they left, I remember looking out the window and being able to see them walk to their car in the parking lot. They were laughing, talking, and enjoying one another. They were returning to their regular lives and to their healthy children, but I was still here counting how long each seizure would last and learning about anti-seizure medication you would never want to have to give your child. Our kids should be learning to roll, not learning how to stop from convulsing. I felt trapped in this story, for life.

As years passed, it became more clear that Rhys would never be typical. We flew to Ottawa to see a specialized genetic and metabolic doctor who was able to diagnose Rhys with a very rare genetic mutation in addition to cortical vision impairment and epileptic encephalopathy. He was the 118th in the world to be diagnosed with a mutated KCNQ2 gene. At the time, the doctors knew almost nothing about it other than that he would have a global developmental delay and may have seizures for the rest of his life.

At first, I went into full offense mode, doing everything I could for him. I tried Reiki, Quantum-Touch, naturopathy, Craniosacral therapy, MEDEK therapy, chiropractic therapy, physiotherapy... the list goes on. I thought if I could just love him enough and try everything I could, he would be okay. Each month that he missed milestones, I felt a level of grief beyond measure. The doctors didn't have a long-term prognosis for him; there was no path to follow. I didn't know any other mothers of kids who had special needs. In fact, I would go on to deny that Rhys was a child with special needs for years. I felt as though he was sick and was going to get better.

As Rhys grew, I grew. I learned how to manage the challenges of feeling left out of regular life. I noticed that we were invited out to gatherings and parties less and less. It was probably in part because I was too over-whelmed to reciprocate and plan anything myself and also because Rhys was falling so far behind his peers; we had no friends for him. While the other kids were saying their first words and feeding themselves cute bite-size lunches, Rhys was still learning how to hold up his own head and try to recognize me as his own mum.

Unbeknownst to me, my marriage was crumbling along with my dream of the perfect family. My husband was slowly pulling away, and with the stress of a medically fragile child, I thought it was just part of what we were going through. Apparently, it wasn't. I had to find a way to cope on my own because I no longer fit in anywhere and was less and less sure what my role in life was meant to be.

I felt like I was in a place where I felt like I couldn't get any lower. I knew I needed to change something, but I was so foggy I couldn't see how to do it, so I zeroed in on small changes.

I started to spend less time focusing on what was wrong and what was out of my control, and I started to focus on what I could change and enjoy. I improved my nutrition and exercise routine, and I learned how to run. Within five weeks, I trained for my first 10k. Finally, it was something that I was able to start and finish, and it made me incredibly proud.

When it comes to parenting, the days are long, but the years are short. At the time, I never really bought into that proverb. All I knew is that my days were incredibly, incredibly tiring, long, and lonely. The future was so very daunting. On average, it costs $100,000 per year to have a child with special needs, and they will be dependent on you for life—not eighteen years or so, like his brother, but until the day I die.

Enough of that. Just enough already. I was so over feeling alone, and I decided to focus on what made me feel great and collected people in my life who also wanted to feel better. Somehow, focusing on the positive allowed everything else in my life to shine brighter.

I started to share my story on social media long before it was a thing. In fact, some people thought I was actually having a breakdown because I was so open about my life. I wanted to connect with others, and I joined a local Facebook group for mothers of kids with special needs. One day, I decided to invite all 224 members to my house. Talk about going out on a limb—I didn't know these women, but I wanted to. I am so glad I hosted that party because on that warm night in July, eight women showed up. We connected, exchanged stories, and laughed, and it became a monthly occurrence.

As I searched to surround myself with positive women I could relate to, I didn't always find mums who thought like I did. I wanted to be with women who looked for the solution, not those who wallowed in the lack thereof. Understandably, they were all in different phases of grief, and some could only see the pain. I was always so hopeful, but each time I saw kids who were much younger than Rhys do things he could never do, it felt like a small death of what could have been. I listened to the typical children yammer on in that adorable language kids have, knowing I would never hear Rhys call me Mumma or even Mum. As those kids beg their parents, asking for toys they wanted, Rhys would never even allow me to make eye contact with him so that he could ask for what he wanted.

I had two options. I could have hope and possibly disappointment, or I could choose to have no hope and decide I will forever be unhappy because life didn't turn out like I thought it would.

It wasn't until it dawned on me that the sooner I accepted Rhys for who he was, the sooner I was going to feel joy. I wasn't going to be able to change him, so I needed to change myself. When I finally recognized that he would likely never walk on his own, I felt a sense of relief. I could start to see into the future and realized we needed a kick-ass wheelchair in electric blue to match our SUV. Even though Rhys doesn't communicate verbally, his laugh tells an incredible story and lights up the room. It's okay that we can't take Rhys to ski lessons or hockey on the weekends. And it's okay that there are only adults at Rhys's birthday parties, and it's totally okay that we are on a different path. Rhys shines a light of hope for so many, and he is so very loved.

The first six weeks of the pandemic passed, and it became clear to Canadians that kids were not going to go back to school anytime soon, that the plastic partitions were not going to come down between the checkouts, and that sports and programs were a thing of the past. I felt a sense of calm. I didn't have to load Rhys up in the car or worry about slipping on the ice as I carried him. We could stay inside. All-day clinic appointments at the hospital were swapped with twenty-minute video conferences in an environment where I could take notes at my desk and properly hear what the doctor had to say. I no longer had to go to work events; they were delivered to me right through my monitor. It seemed as though there wasn't a sense of comparison anymore because everyone's hair was shaggy, no one worried about their manicures, and suddenly, even talking about it seemed frivolous.

I loved it. My boys were with me, and I built a new routine. I had accepted what was going on in the world, and I knew almost instantly that I wasn't waiting for it to end. In fact, I knew that it was never going to go back to the way it used to be. Finally, the typical world had caught up to Rhys's world. Everyone else had to stop attending the programs, the tennis, the playdates, the social engagements, or even to be able to walk into a store freely—we were all on the same playing field, and I felt empowered. These restrictions had been placed on us the moment Rhys was born. Whether it was an IV pole, the number of times he vomited on himself in a given day, or just the fact that the venue is not wheelchair accessible, we always had to consider everything before we could just get up and go.

Rhys spent the first twelve weeks of his life in the hospital. I can remember a night during that time when my sister came to visit me at about 11:00 p.m. We walked through the dim hallways, and I cried. Neither of us knew what my future held with Rhys, and I couldn't even articulate what it might look like, let alone bear to live it. But I did.

I had to say goodbye to my old life and the vision of family that I used to have and trade it in for this new one that I never asked for. I didn't take it day by day; I took it minute by minute. Each step I took, I was a little bit stronger. I tripped a ton. Even though I fell down often, I kept showing up and smiling as much as I could along the way. Have you ever noticed what happens when you smile at someone with a full, genuine smile? They can't help themselves and almost instantly smile back.

I found my superpower, and I know exactly what I would bring to my team during a zombie apocalypse. This year, you will certainly find your superpower too.

"There is a crack in everything; that's how the light gets in." – Leonard Cohen

About Natalie Boese

Natalie Boese is a lifestyle and digital organization expert who empowers busy professionals to reduce overwhelm and save time by creating simple systems for their health, productivity, and planning.

Natalie's professional career began working for the largest advertising agencies in the world. It included owning her own home decor importing business before finding her truest business love in teaching businesses and individuals how to use Apple products to enhance their lives. Her clients have included some of the world's largest private equity investors, as well as everyday people who want to reduce overwhelm and save time.

Natalie lives in Toronto with her two boys, one with severe special needs who challenges her every day to stay healthy and organized and has inspired her motto of "Eat, Move, Live, Simply."

www.natalieboese.com | natalie@natalieboese.com | IG: @natboese

CHAPTER 7

Learn How to Learn

by Dr. Christine Manukyan

"Maybe the journey isn't so much about becoming anything. Maybe it's about un-becoming everything that isn't really you so you can be who you were meant to be in the first place."

– PAULO COELHO

In the midst of a global pandemic, with unemployment rates rising daily and uncertainty everywhere, I made the crazy decision to leave my job, my security, and my reputation as a hospital clinical pharmacist. While many lives changed throughout 2020, I had the luxury of changing mine by choice.

I was tired of choosing between my family and my career, and I hit my breaking point. I was on the front lines as a medical worker, with no ability to work from home and no days off, as my young children struggled with the new challenge of online schooling, no social interactions, and quarantine.

I'd been a part-time parent for a decade. This was *my* time to make up for the ten years of memories and connection I'd given up for a successful career that no longer fulfilled me. Five years earlier, I had begun a journey to un-become the person I was raised to be in my personal and professional life. Leaving my job and leaning into my family was the right choice to continue to *become* the person I am now.

I was born and raised in Yerevan, Armenia. In the 1980s, life was quite different back home. Women were seen as people without a voice who dedicated their lives to motherhood, and the only acceptable option was staying home with children. Women were not seen as role models, and those who pursued careers were judged for prioritizing themselves instead of choosing family first. I grew up watching my mom and all the women in my life make decisions about how they "had to stay home," and I heard many of them say they wished they could work part time while still being a mom.

Inspired by the American dream of more opportunities and a better life, my family immigrated to America when I was sixteen years old. As a teenager, acclimating to a new country was lonely, painful, and overwhelming. I missed my life, my friends, and my home country! I struggled with adjusting to the societal norms of a foreign place where I had no roots, and I was terrified because I spoke very little English. I struggled with making friends and interacting comfortably with others.

I felt lost and out of place. I turned to food for comfort, and before I knew it, as my weight increased, my self-esteem decreased. I felt ashamed of my physical appearance and constantly judged by others, and I missed out on so many social activities and opportunities. My habits didn't change with age. I was addicted to the sugar, carbs, caffeine, and fast food we could afford, living paycheck to paycheck on government assistance.

Watching my mom work two jobs to provide for our family while going to school in the evenings, I realized I had to do something to contribute. I had to let go of the norms of a young Armenian woman without a voice and start helping my mom to lessen the struggle. Just months after arriving in America, I was hired to sell menswear at Sears, barely speaking English.

During my first week at work, I approached an older gentleman who seemed lost and asked how I could help him. He was looking for a burgundy polo shirt. I had no clue what "burgundy" was or what a polo shirt looked like, but I was determined to help him out. I asked more questions, trying to figure out where I should start. At least I knew he was looking for a shirt. I made conversation as we wandered around the department store looking for a burgundy polo shirt.

We finally found the shirt for him, and he rewarded me with the best compliment of my day: He said he had enjoyed shopping with me and appreciated the time I took to talk to him. I felt seen and in a positive light, something I hadn't experienced since I'd moved to the U.S. I knew I could do this.

It's a feeling and memory that stayed with me forever, the moment I realized I have to and *can* make life no matter what the circumstances. The realization that I can figure it out if I have a strong desire to reach my goals has stayed with me.

As an Armenian woman, I had been subconsciously conditioned to put everyone else's needs before mine. If an Armenian woman takes care of herself before taking care of others, she is judged for being selfish and not being committed to her family. Armenian women are raised to tolerate abuse, keep the peace, and remain voiceless as if our dreams don't matter.

Growing up in Armenia, I had no role models who were female CEOs or entrepreneurs. Without even realizing it, I was growing up to believe that I couldn't dream big. Most Armenian women became teachers, caregivers, and bankers; some became lawyers, doctors, or accountants. Being an Armenian CEO was unthinkable in Armenia when I was growing up in the 80s, even more so than the gender gap in American roles of power.

I had to learn quickly that I was no longer in Armenia, and now, I had more opportunities, like the ability to pursue a career in pharmacy in my twenties. I was lovingly nicknamed Wonder Woman in my pharmacy school professional fraternity, Phi Delta Chi, because others saw me as a leader and someone with strength and potential.

Shortly after graduating from pharmacy school and finishing my two-year residency at Ohio State, I moved back to California and started the next chapter of my life. I was the happiest I had ever been in my life as a newlywed, especially when I became a mother when I was thirty years old. But my back-to-back pregnancies caused more weight gain, and my health spiraled out of control. As a new mother, I was focused on my family, work, and others, and I forgot about self-love and self-care. I became morbidly obese and saw my health declining as my career was blooming. I had no energy, and I was unable to be fully present with my kids.

In 2015, I went to my annual physical at age thirty-five, and my doctor informed me that if I didn't change my lifestyle, I was highly likely to have a heart attack by the age of forty. I was stunned. I felt humiliated, blaming myself because I should have known better. I felt lost, like I lost part of my identity. I knew I had to make changes, but I had no clue where to start. I just knew there had to be a better way to get healthy without pharmaceuticals. I was overwhelmed and terrified at the thought of not being around to watch my children grow!

That weekend, I gave myself the best Mother's Day present: I committed to rewriting my story. I learned about functional medicine and began focusing more on the root cause of my failing health, learning how to use food as medicine. I also realized my health was connected to my highly stressful career, so I made a decision to step down from my current management position and work as a clinical staff pharmacist. I had to focus on what mattered to me the most: my health and my family. Putting aside my ego and title to focus on a healthy lifestyle was incredibly challenging, but it was one of the best decisions I have ever made.

I realized the power of making decisions and how one decision can simply transform your life. Who would have thought I would lose over 100 pounds through intermittent fasting, exercise, and incorporating functional medicine into my daily routine? It gave me a boost of self-confidence that allowed me to step out onstage as a fitness competitor, dressed as Wonder Woman, to empower other women to say *yes* to themselves, and to represent what's possible when you take consistent action every single day.

While training for my fitness show, I had to work so hard to let go of negative noise and comments. Other Armenian women I considered to be my friends challenged me, made me feel ashamed by making that decision. Deciding intentionally to go from being obese to becoming a bodybuilding athlete had the opposite feelings for me. It exemplified strength, commitment, and dedication to accomplish such a huge goal. I could inspire other women and inspire my own daughter to chase her dreams and not let others dictate what she can or can't do.

In the years since that obesity diagnosis, my weight loss journey, and transforming myself into my own version of Wonder Woman, I learned how much I have un-become, and I began to focus on the next goal I would love to accomplish. I fell in love with the idea of the unknown and living life to the fullest even though I didn't have all the answers. This feeling scared me but also excited me to know what's possible. This became part of my identity: Once I reached a huge goal, I would always think of the next one.

I was hungry for growth and possibilities and living my life on autopilot wasn't what I wanted to settle for. I started to realize how much it hurt when I had to miss out on quality time with my family. I was hitting another burnout point in my life at age thirty-nine, thinking it was a midlife crisis. I didn't like who I was becoming. I spent more time commuting to work than I spent with my kids, and I started asking myself, "Is this it? Is this really what I imagined myself doing?"

I soon found myself at a company event, listening to a mentor of mine speak. I felt like she was speaking directly to me. She made me realize how unhappy I was as a part-time mom with a full-time career. My family was getting my leftovers, and they didn't deserve that.

At that moment, on August 13, 2019, I wrote myself a letter titled "The Power of Vision Casting." I started seeing the power of manifestation and creating vision boards that summarized my ideal life. On my vision board, I wanted to retire at age forty and become a full-time mom working from home and being my own boss, helping others reach their health and wealth goals. I came home from the event and told the kids that the following year they would not have to stay in school so late, that I would be working from home so I could pick them up as soon as school ended. This was a huge goal for me. I didn't know *how* I was going to accomplish it, but my *why* was so strong that I knew I would figure out a way.

I saw my health decline as I was living a very stressful life. I decided it was time to take on an item from my bucket list, which was to run a marathon for my fortieth birthday. Just the idea of running the Los Angeles Marathon on March 8, 2020, scared me. However, I could envision myself crossing the finish line on International Women's Day, celebrating all women.

Letting go of the feeling of the unknown and owning the feeling of possibilities was a reminder that I am capable of accomplishing this milestone. I reminded myself that I have a Wonder Woman mindset, and I am *unstoppable*. I was running this race for the scared and unhealthy girl I once was, for my Armenian sisters who could not imagine such a feat. This race was a symbol to me of overcoming all my life's challenges: immigration, poor health, and insecurity. Running this race was part of un-becoming me and *reinventing* myself. Little did I know I would be making history in the last race before the COVID-19 pandemic lockdown.

How can two completely different feelings—happy excitement and suffocating anxiety—be experienced in the same day? All of a sudden, March 2020 had become the most difficult time of our lives. We were left with no childcare and no options for working from home.

Like many others, I learned how to slow down during the pandemic. I focused on what mattered the most at that time: taking care of our children and managing our health. I returned again and again to one of my favorite quotes by Mark Twain: "The two most important days in your life are the day you are born and the day you find out why." I focused on leading with passion and purpose, helping others transform their health without pharmaceuticals, and incorporating functional medicine into their lifestyles. I started to ask myself, "How I can pivot?" and "How I can have the best of both worlds?" so I didn't have to choose between career and family.

I had to find a way to match my corporate income while working from home and taking care of the kids. In order to do that, I had to think outside of the box; I had to focus on investing in myself so I could find ways to work from home if the pandemic was going to last longer. After a lot of thinking and reinventing myself, I found a way to once again un-become the traditional clinical pharmacist I was, who had been trained in acute care hospital settings for thirteen years and to shift focus to preventive medicine using functional medicine. This was a huge decision because I was not surrounded by others who have done this before, so I had to *learn how to learn* as I was stepping out of traditional medicine to holistic medicine. I made a decision to start a brand-new journey by hiring a business coach and joining a mastermind to help me use my skills and training to build my own virtual functional medicine practice.

I saw an opportunity in my profession that many haven't thought about. I saw an opportunity for growth and the opportunity for an exit strategy if the pandemic was going to last longer than we thought. Creating my own functional medicine virtual practice during the global pandemic became my goal so I could walk away from corporate and I no longer have to choose between family and career.

I committed to the solution—working from home, being my own boss without sacrificing my income by launching my own functional medicine practice amidst the pandemic. Once again, I felt so accomplished having created something without knowing how it would happen and letting the desire to rewrite my story guide my way. I knew I would have many challenges along the way, and I was okay with that. It was a bold decision, and it was something the real-life Wonder Woman would do.

I continued working limited hours on the weekends at the hospital and started my virtual practice in May of 2020 in addition to my job. I realized that our childcare situation wasn't perfect, but we made it work until one day, I was informed that my work schedule could not be accommodated any longer and that I had to go back to work full time starting June. Telling the kids that I had to hire a nanny—a complete stranger—from an agency so I could go back to work was one of the hardest days of the pandemic.

Both kids cried and asked, "Why are you leaving us? What if this person hurts us? What if we get sick? Why is work more important than us?" I cried as I tried to comfort them, saying, "Everything will be okay," and "We will get through this together." It was so hard that I couldn't sleep for days, and I drank more wine than normal to help me relax and forget temporarily about the reality of our situation. It was so hard knowing I had no other options but to leave the kids and go back to work full time.

A month passed, and I found myself feeling guilty and doubted about the decision I made. Just in time, when I was hitting another rock bottom, I made a decision to attend a virtual event by Tony Robbins, "Unleash the Power Within (UPW)." My kids saw me go through my transformation and breakthrough. They heard me speak my goals out loud that I will find a way to work from home so I don't have to choose between family and career. This event changed my life; it gave me *clarity* on what I wanted to do because I was surrounded by others who were *hungry* for growth as much as I was.

During this event, I met someone very special, an incredible female CEO who became my idol. I was so inspired by Tony Robbins's interview with Sara Blakely, inventor of Spanx. I got chills listening to her story. I was moved by her passion and purpose to make a difference in this world and support other female entrepreneurs. I found my calling and the guts to pursue my passion and purpose, to help other women rewrite their stories and become the best version of themselves. It was just the perfect timing in my life to *reclaim* my purpose and focus on making a difference in this world.

After this event, I hired a fashion consultant for a new fashion technology product idea I was committed to bringing to life, got accepted to a Berkeley Skydeck accelerator program for my startup company, STORRIE™, and turned in my two-week notice on exactly the same date I wrote my vision casting letter to myself a year ago. Becoming a corporate dropout during the pandemic for my fortieth birthday was a sign to never doubt what I am capable of doing. All my life's challenges prepared me to un-become who I had become, let go of the old me, and make room for the person I was meant to be in the first place.

Leaving my career as a clinical pharmacist for thirteen years to pursue my purpose and passion as a full-time mom, entrepreneur, startup founder, Functional Medicine Practitioner, and business coach was my calling. This pandemic made me realize how much we can do with our lives if we have a burning desire to pursue our goals. Walking away from security and moving forward without the answers, which goes against my life-long pharmacist training of doing the research *before* taking action, was terrifying but also so exciting. I now have the opportunity to dream again: Write a book, launch the STORRIE™ Podcast and STORRIE™ sports bra, and live my life with intention and purpose. I now know I can create my own reality.

"If you don't create your reality, your reality will create you." – Lizzie West

Take a few minutes and write your vision casting letter to yourself, describing your ideal life. Then, as if it's already happened, write how you were able to let go of the fear and *redefine* your life, reinvent your-self, and *reclaim* your purpose. **Give yourself permission** to do things differently.

I'll leave you with my motto: "I believe everyone deserves a second chance to rewrite their story and become the best version of themselves."

Until then, live with passion.

Dr. Christine Manukyan

About Dr. Christine Manukyan

Dr. Christine Manukyan is a Functional Medicine Practitioner, business coach, author, speaker, top-rated STORRIE™ Podcast host, and mother of two. Prior to becoming an entrepreneur, she spent thirteen years in corporate America as a Clinical Pharmacist with various leadership roles. After experiencing her own health transformation with functional medicine, losing 100+ pounds, and becoming a natural bodybuilding athlete and marathon runner, she found her true calling, empowering others to reach their health goals without pharmaceuticals. Dr. Christine has helped more than 300 clients transform their health.

She is a frequent speaker on holistic lifestyle choices, creating a virtual business, a founder and entrepreneur mindset, and creating multiple income streams. She's spoken in front of audiences numbering 15,000+ and has been recognized globally for her entrepreneurial achievement and dedication.

Her magazine features include PharmaSis Magazine for female pharma-cist entrepreneurs, health and wellness publications, and she is a BRAINZ Magazine Executive Contributor, having received BRAINZ 500 Global recognition. In 2021, she's bringing a revolutionary product to market as a startup partnered with the UC Berkeley Skydeck accelerator and incubator.

Dr. Christine is passionate about helping burned-out medical profes-sionals build and scale a profitable virtual practice to have more quality time with their loved ones doing what fulfills their lives. She believes everyone deserves a second chance to rewrite their stories and become the best versions of themselves.

www.drchristinemanukyan.com | DrChristine@storrie.co | IG: @dr.christine.manukyan

CHAPTER 8

A Pandemic Journal

by Michelle Demaree

*"You owe it to yourself to become everything
you have ever dreamed of being."*

– EVAN SANDERS

Everyone began 2020 with high hopes and dreams of a stellar year, yet when the pandemic began, the world closed down. Businesses, banks, schools, airports, parks, restaurants—the physical world became a ghost town. As the CEO of a global luxury diamond consulting business, I had never planned for a worldwide shutdown. I asked myself: Would clients stop purchasing engagement rings now that Rodeo Drive and Fifth Avenue were closed? Would proposals pause, and would high net worth clientele halt their love-filled spending habits?

Turns out, love did not close down, and the business I created five years prior was perfectly positioned for 2020.

These are my top three takeaways that enabled me to create a unique and prolific business that flourished during the pandemic.

If they go left, you go right

Seven years ago, I left the glamorous world of retail after selling millions in high jewelry for esteemed jewelry houses, including *Harry Winston, Tiffany & Company,* and *Van Cleef & Arpels.* That departure was meant to be temporary to start a family, but when my daughter was one, I felt a calling to establish a service that did not yet exist in the luxury marketplace.

What began as a lightning flash of an idea during a women's retreat grew to be a nearly completely virtual luxury client-driven business model that offered the total dream: better diamond options with more personalized service and the ability for me to generate income with a balanced business that also allowed me to be at home and raise my daughter. Combined with bespoke ring-making, my idea allowed every couple's unique love story to be realized, including proposal planning services for their special moment.

From years in high-end sales, I knew a personalized connection and a high-touch concierge service was needed for such a special purchase. This business not only made sense, but it also worked for my life and my goals of wanting to be with my daughter and work on my terms. I had little capital to invest in a brick-and-mortar business, so a lean overhead model was the winner.

The diamond industry is currently run mostly by men, most of whom seemed fairly indifferent to what the ring stood for and more interested in numbers, costs, and beating their competitors than love stories and the emotional value of pieces that would become family heirlooms. It was a race to the bottom that needed to be up-leveled through a business model driven by love and connection.

Although many in the industry told me the business model would never work, I found the strength to listen to that voice in my heart that said, "*Keep going and keep building.*" I established my online high jewelry service and website and started servicing clients around the world. I started with just one client and one wholesale connection, and over the years, through compound clienteling (the power of one client turning into millions in revenue) and unparalleled customer service offering the best experience and top-quality rings, it's grown to a multi-million-dollar revenue business with diamond contacts in every city around the world.

I went from having little visibility and no press to the New York Times asking to do a profile write-up about my role as a ring concierge. *That was a game-changer.*

Cast a wide net for lead generation

Business was booming in 2019, but I was relying very heavily on one platform for nearly all of my leads outside of referrals. I was all-in on Instagram, and when the algorithm changed, my leads disappeared. I went from getting ten leads a week to one lead every other week—overnight.

Business came to a screeching halt, and I was scrambling to try and find the same leads on Instagram by paying a boatload that weeks prior had fallen onto my grid so easily. Instagram had changed their entire advertisement and engagement algorithm (similar to when Facebook did) so businesses would have to spend significantly more to target their audience.

I learned quickly that I could not depend on one platform or source for lead generation, even if it is working. I realized I must diversify because things can change at any moment for any reason. With that lesson learned, I set out to diversify where my business came from. I went all-in on SEO, Pinterest, YouTube, FB ads, influencer partnerships, affiliate ambassadorships, and Google ads.

SEO was a long-term game, but the longer you keep at it, the more it works for you. A year later, I'm on page one of Google. When the pandemic began in March and jewelry stores all over the world closed, I was perfectly positioned to succeed because I had cast a wide net for leads online. And I was offering the exact product and service (but more personalized) as the closed-down name-brand stores on Rodeo Drive, and the sales came in.

Never F*cking Give Up

Pandemic or not, the path of an entrepreneur is a rewarding roller coaster of ups and downs, twists and turns, failures and successes. I may have done well during the pandemic, but in years prior, I had some really difficult months. I was perfectly positioned for the pandemic *only* because I hit a wall the year prior and made the necessary changes to continue and pivot as a business. No entrepreneur ever knows exactly what to do. You try different things out until you find something that works, and then you double down.

On this roller coaster, you'll have days you'll be on top of the world, flooded with endorphins from a killer sale or huge win, and feel like you are on the verge of your next big break. Other days you will be sitting in the car eating McDonald's, crying, saying, "What am I doing!?" (I know a friend who may have done that a time or two.) Being an entrepreneur means you are building something new and problem solving in a way that takes you on a zigzag "choose your own adventure" of mistakes that lead to wins, and it is literally the only way to do it. So the rule of being an

Entrepreneur is: ***Never f*cking give up.* If you do not give up, you cannot fail.** *Resilience, creativity, and perseverance are more powerful than any skill set you could have.*

My path to my current success was not easy, but I succeeded because I didn't give up...

I started with one small diamond sale five years ago. Now, five years later, I do $3 million in revenue.

I started with one wholesaler as a contact in the diamond industry (this substantially limits the inventory you can pull for clientele). Every year I went to the trade show, I would knock on doors, call new businesses, and introduce myself, and over time, I am as plugged into the global diamond market as one could hope to be.

I hired four marketing/advertising "expert professionals" who generated zero in online sales for me (I target ultra-high-net-worth buyers spending $35,000 to $350,000 per ring). I spent tens of thousands and got nothing. I did not give up. The fifth person I hired killed it, and within one week started generating two to three legitimate leads for my business. I have him on full time.

I hired two PR companies who got me zero press. The third person I hired (from Upwork) landed me the NY Times within two months, and it continued from there.

Three years ago, I had zero press—zero. I now am in the NY Times, LA Times, Yahoo Finance, People, Pop Sugar, Modern Luxury, E News, Us Weekly, and more. It's a long list, and once you get one or two, you can leverage that press for more.

I partnered with more than ten influencers, gave them thousands in diamonds to promote, and barely broke even with the sales it generated.

I did not give up. The last influencer celebrity who actually purchased something from me broke the internet with my ring, and it generated several massive publications about my business in four days (People, Cosmopolitan, Today, Us Weekly, CNN, Pop Sugar, and more).

The biggest takeaway is that when unexpected things happen, be able to pivot, change quickly, be resourceful, and think outside the box. Most importantly, don't get down on yourself and your ideas or compare yourself to someone else as the ideal of where you should be. Every experience is there to teach you something, positive or negative. Take the lesson, use it as feedback, and don't give up. Enjoy the wild, unexpected, and exhilarating ride of being an entrepreneur.

That dream was planted in your heart for a reason—so go out and get it!

xoxo, Michelle Demaree

About Michelle Demaree

Michelle Demaree is the Founder of Miss Diamond Ring, an international luxury diamond consultancy based on the West Coast. Her passion for artistically capturing every couple's unique love story through her bespoke Love Legacy rings has established her as the New Standard in Ring Shopping in the diamond industry, redefining the engagement ring process for couples.

She has been featured in *The New York Times, Los Angeles Times, Modern Luxury, Page Six Style, Yahoo, US Weekly, Entertainment Tonight, Life & Style, The American Dream* and is being featured in the *Rolls Royce exclusive 2021 Best of the Best: Royal Edition.* In 2019, The New York Times took an interest in her unique business of curating six-figure rings for couples around the world through her Virtual Diamond Atelier Service.

Tapping into the business model of love, connection, and alignment, Michelle has flipped the switch in the luxury, transactional, and male-dominated diamond industry. Over the past six years, she evolved her international boutique female-owned business into a highly personalized experience for couples seeking unique, one-of-a-kind engagement rings that honor their love story at the highest level. She utilizes her Rodeo Drive network, expertise, and craftsmanship to create the highest-quality experience for her celebrity and UHNW clientele, giving them a ring and an experience like no other.

www.missdiamondring.com | michelle@missdiamondring.com | IG: @missdiamondring

CHAPTER 9

The Magic of Trusting Your Gut and Following Your Heart

by Amanda Perna

"Go confidently in the direction of your dreams;
live the life you've imagined."

– HENRY DAVID THOREAU

Life can be hard, even in the best of times. You constantly try to make things better and take the next step. Some things work, some things don't. When things aren't working out, it can be really unclear if you're even on the right path. But one thing is clear: When you are on the right path, it makes it a lot easier to keep moving in the right direction.

Sometimes, an obstacle is dropped in your path that makes it hard to see what's in front of you and makes you question everything—your goals, your desires, your purpose in life—even when you had previously thought you had it all figured out. The COVID-19 pandemic that swept across the globe in 2020 made everyone stop and think. If life is hard in the best of times, what do you do in the worst?

You hear a lot of people talk about "finding your purpose," figuring out what you are "meant to do." And so many of us try to force ourselves to find our purpose and create something out of this feeling of necessity. What if your real purpose is right inside you, and you are just listening to all the outside voices instead of the one inside? What if you follow your dreams and passions and can have everything you have ever imagined and some? What if, instead of forcing yourself to make plans, you just jumped in and started?

What if I told you that you could do all of this while the world is upside down, in the middle of a pandemic, and you have no idea which way to turn? You can do it! How do I know this? Because I did it. I stumbled upon it at a time when I wasn't even looking for it. I was just by being open to what was right in front of me. Open your eyes, feel what's in your heart, jump right in, and you too can do everything you dream of and much, much more!

I am a recovering perfectionist, a Type A personality that loves lists, guidelines, and making plans. But the truth is that every time I have listened to my gut and jumped in, I have been so much more successful than when I make all the lists and plans and write the rules. I was the annoying kid in school who needed an A+. Yes, you heard that right: an A+. An A- was the equivalent of an F to me. I was going to school to be a doctor of psychology so I could help save the world one person at a time.

My whole life was changed by one sewing class. It led to another and another and then me double majoring. Then I got it in my head that I was moving to New York City to become a fashion designer, eventually dropping psychology altogether. People said I was insane to throw away my safe career plan, but I trusted my heart and made it happen.

I worked at two of the biggest American fashion houses of all time. After a few years of working what I thought was my dream job with a 401k, benefits, and a steady paycheck, something told me to start my own business. Once again, I went against all the advice I was given, and I cashed in that 401k and started my own business. I figured people invest in stocks and real estate; I would invest in the one thing I could sort of control—myself.

Fast forward to the beginning of the year 2020. I have a thriving business with employees who rely on me, stores that sell my products, clients who come to me for custom gowns, and brands that partner with me to create in-store activations and other content. Compared to a lot of other careers, I know these things are, in the grand scheme, not that important, but doing them well is important to me, and I take these responsibilities seriously.

I want to be the best boss, and I strive to provide the best products and customer service to my clients and partners. Going in, the plan was to make 2020 the best year ever in my business. In February, I flew from Palm Beach to New York for an amazing week. I met with brands, publishers, and magazines (including an acquaintance at Good Housekeeping) about working on collaboration, and I left feeling on top of the world!

March rolled around, and I traveled to California for a two-week business trip with my family in tow. I went to a conference where I met brands to collaborate with (including Pinterest) and amazing entrepreneurs. Next, I proceeded to an incredible influencer weekend. We went to some huge meetings and a tradeshow to start selling our products to even more retailers. 2020 was looking to live up to the plan!

Then the unexpected happened while we are out in California. They declared a state of emergency for something called COVID-19. I had been hearing about this virus for a few months at this point, as many of our overseas partners were battling the virus, but I never imagined it would come here and cause everything to shut down. Our bubble quickly burst as we went to the abandoned LAX Airport to return to Florida.

At this point, we knew we needed to self-quarantine for two weeks just in case, so I told my employees I would be out for an additional two weeks to keep everyone safe.

While self-quarantining after the trip, we received the news that our town was going into lockdown. Clients started canceling their gowns, stores started canceling orders, and events started getting postponed.

In normal times, I'm typically surrounded by the most amazing people at my office and during events. I am constantly on the go, and I am almost never home. The first few days stuck at home, I thought, "Okay, this is a needed break after weeks of business travel." Then another week went by, and I had a feeling of hopelessness, depression, and a lack of inspiration that I've never felt in my entire life. I had no work, no money coming in, and we had to take a look at all of our personal and business assets and expenses to figure out how long we could survive. I was racking my brain trying to figure out how to keep my team employed and able to pay their bills since I knew we could only last paying them for so long.

While sitting home, crying, and watching the news, I was moved by a story. A nurse was on TV begging people to help sew face masks. She said they had one mask for weeks on end and that the health care workers were getting sick. Without a second thought, I knew that this was what I needed to do. I ran to my studio, grabbed all the fabric I had for summer dresses, and promised myself I was going to sew masks to donate. I made a goal I knew I could manage—I would sew 100 masks to donate. It was a small goal, but every bit helps, and I started researching.

If I was going to give these masks to frontline workers, I knew that I had to make them as protective as possible. I reached out to doctors, surgeons and, of course, searched the internet. I started to make prototypes to see which were the best patterns, materials, and methods to make them.

I got to sewing and posted on my social media asking if anyone else wanted to help sew. I made a video about how to do it so others could help. Little did I know that it would lead to the local news stations jumping in to share my story. All of a sudden, our email was bombarded by the public also asking to purchase masks.

My goal was just to help as many people as possible; I had no intention of profiting. And then it hit me! I could start a buy-one-donate-one program and be able to help keep frontline workers and the public safe while keeping my team in their jobs!

I called a friend who helps with the production of our clothes and asked her if she would help. Before you know it, we had our sewing people up and running, gave jobs to their friends, and were online. We had so many requests that we repeatedly had to shut down our website. We set a goal that at the time seemed like a long shot of 1,000 masks—500 to sell and 500 to donate.

Then I got a DM from an editor I had met in February at Good Housekeeping. She saw the video I posted on social media and asked if I would make a video to share with their readers so they could make masks at home as well. I immediately said yes, as there was such a shortage, and masks were becoming mandatory across the country. My husband and I went to my closed studio, filmed the video, and sent it over.

A few days later, we were at home, and my website started going crazy. Every minute we had an order coming through. Our video was live, and people from all over the world were placing orders, so many that we had to turn off our website multiple times because we couldn't keep up with the numbers coming in.

I started getting emails from people on every continent thanking me for helping them sew masks to keep themselves, their loved ones, and their communities safe. I had never, in my entire life, felt so proud or so passionate about anything as I did about making masks with my team to save lives. We donated tens of thousands of masks (and still counting as I write this months later), helping people from health care professionals and other frontline workers to the homeless stay safe.

The first mask-making video I made for Good Housekeeping led to a series of four videos and to me being featured in countless publications and partnering with Pinterest to make fashionable masks. My videos have been viewed by millions of people and were number one in all of Hearst Publications for page views and put on every one of their sites.

If I hadn't just trusted my gut and jumped in to help, I honestly don't know what would have happened to my business, my team, or my family. I truly believe that when you do something for the right reasons, especially in service to others, it comes back tenfold. You have to trust your gut, follow your heart, and all of your dreams will come true. It may not be in the most direct path or one you even have mapped out. Sometimes you have to throw the map out of the window and just trust the light inside of you.

My plans to keep creating products were not abandoned; I was just led on a detour, one that allowed me to help more people than I ever thought possible. This is my story of finding purpose and meaning in my life and career. Yours will be different, but the key is allowing yourself to be open to the opportunities that prevent themselves and finding ways to connect the dots when they do.

I went to an event where I met a person that worked at a place. When the COVID-19 pandemic struck, the connections that came from this one meeting allowed me the opportunity to get in front of millions of people and provide them the information they needed to help themselves and others while also helping my team get through a really tough time and find a purpose!

By remaining flexible, leaving room for magic, and trusting the inner voice that believes in you, you can see everything you imagine become reality. You will see the patterns emerging to confirm that you are on the right track if you are paying attention. Some days are hard, and some-times you may feel lost. There is always a reason, a silver lining, and a purpose for everything we go through.

This idea of openness may seem vague, but there are ways to help keep yourself ready to see the right paths when they present themselves to you. It's all about your mindset, a way of planning without planning. Start by taking the time to think about what you do and don't like to do, what you do and don't want out of life, and how you can be a part of making the world a better place for yourself and others. Think about the types of ideas you would like to pursue, and then make a conscious effort every single day to be open to what life puts in front of you.

It's not an inactive mindset of waiting for a great idea or opportunity to fall out of the sky; it is an active mindset that lets you grab that idea or opportunity instead of letting it float by and disappear into the grave-yard of thoughts that could have led to more. It's about allowing yourself to see the path that will lead you to a fulfilling life purpose instead of wasting time on paths that lead to unhappiness.

There will be times when the path in front of you is so clear and other times that you have no idea how to get through the day. As long as you believe in yourself and continue to push forward in pursuit of sharing your passion and sunshine with the world, there will always be a light at the end of the tunnel.

"There is only one you, and that is your superpower!" – Author unknown

About Amanda Perna

Amanda Perna is a mom, wife, design expert, content creator, speaker, author, illustrator, stylist, and entrepreneur. Loved for her approachability, Amanda's mission is to create joy and spread sunshine wherever she goes.

Amanda first fell in love with fashion during design school at the Fashion Institute of Technology, but she honed her craft while designing for major fashion brands, including Oscar de la Renta and Calvin Klein in New York City. Though she loved learning under the expertise of renowned designers, Amanda's entrepreneurial spirit always called her to begin her own fashion brands.

The House of Perna and Neon Bohemians were born. These brands, the truest reflections of the dynamic sides of Amanda's personality, have been sold internationally to high-end retailers, including Bloomingdale's, Nordstrom, and more! She specializes in creating ethically made products and designs with an eye focused on maximalist style with minimalist waste, always featuring bright colors and bold prints.

In addition to designing for her signature collections, Amanda is a sought-after creative who has styled celebrity clients, films, and notable fashion events. Her partnerships and collaborations have included brands such as Anthropologie, Neiman Marcus, BHLDN, and FabFitFun. As an artist, Amanda has curated her own museum exhibitions, designed whimsical card collections for Hallmark Signature, and is a four-time featured artist at Art Basel.

Since appearing on two seasons of Project Runway, Amanda's work has been internationally recognized in hundreds of press mentions, and she is a well-respected and prominent television personality, co-hosting a weekly morning show as well as numerous national guest spots. She's a popular content creator and collaborator, working with companies like Hearst Publications, Pinterest, Good Housekeeping, and Woman's Day.

Amanda became a best-selling published author in 2019 with her first children's book, F is for Fashion, an illustrated book of fashion ABCs.

Amanda is incredibly involved in her local community and donates time, money, and resources to philanthropic causes. She serves on the board of the Greater Delray Beach Chamber of Commerce and the Achievement Center for Children and Families.

Above all else, Amanda is a firm believer that you can have anything and everything you want if you're willing to work for it. Life is too short not to follow your dreams!

www.amandaperna.com | info@amandaperna.com |
IG: @theamandaperna

CHAPTER 10

Granting Myself Grace and Pivoting My Perspective

By Dr. Sarah Mitchell

"The pandemic happened FOR me, not TO me."

– DR. SARAH MITCHELL

The pandemic came, and my priorities shifted. With two elementary school-aged children to suddenly home school, I had no time to work on my business. My husband is in big tech and makes more money than me, and as a self-employed entrepreneur with flexibility, it became my role to be with the children by default.

At first, I didn't really mind. My business had slowed down by sixty percent, and I had a bit more time. I've always been a nurturing sort, and my kids are important to me. I also looked at the circumstances as a new opportunity to understand the difficulties my son had been having at school. In third grade, we'd been having school refusal since the fall.

The time to be close to him to observe how he managed with school lessons and his learning habits was an opportunity. It was soon easy to see the struggles he was having, which gave me deeper empathy and understanding toward him. As the weeks went by, I kept lowering my standards for school and focusing more on the kids' mental health than scholastic performance. I started looking at the pandemic as an opportunity to *unschool* him and to be undoing the negative associations he'd developed for school due to the negative responses he'd been receiving from his teachers.

I let my toenails guide me. My nails were damaged from having pedicures constantly for over a year. Now with the polish removed, I could see the damage, and I had all the time in the world to watch them grow out. I used this slow growth as a measure for our unschooling process. Only time could heal things.

As the weeks rolled on, I learned to grant myself grace, to focus each day on what will make me happy in this moment, to not be a victim of my circumstance. Yes, I could complain that the kids were driving me nuts, and this was hard. I could complain about the sharp decline in business as the world held its breath in April and wondered what would happen next. Or I could pivot my thoughts to something else and do something physical or mental for myself.

I learned to trust myself, to remember months in the past when business had dropped off and the following months when it had rebounded. I'd learned to trust my instincts about my son's displeasure, angst, and tears about going to school even though the teachers told me he was fine once he got there. As the traffic on the streets decreased and slow living increased, I learned to be more mindful and listen more to my heart and my instincts. It became much easier to let go of societal norms of what learning and being should look like. I began attaching my self-worth and happiness to how well I was caring for myself and others rather than my monthly revenue.

My family got used to having more time on our hands, to developing new rituals and habits. I started a new morning routine, getting up extra early, enjoying a cup of tea in the quiet, and going for a run with my neighbor. We would run and listen to NPR news or Brene Brown podcasts, expanding our minds, wondering what the world would look like in the future. It was fabulous. I was able to let go of what I thought I should be doing, and the projects that I'd had in store for my business were put on the back burner, granting myself grace to coast. What became important was moving our bodies every day and the children's mental health. We surrendered.

And then fall came, and they announced school would continue to be online. I already knew we'd be moving my son to a smaller private school, which would better accommodate his needs. The pandemic had helped me see how his struggles were legitimate and needed extra care despite what others were saying. While the thought of paying for private school wasn't exciting, especially given the slump in my biz, I knew in my heart we had to try something new for him, and I was getting really good at trusting my instincts.

My daughter tried online public school for three weeks and cried every day. Life's too short to cry every day, so we dipped further into our savings and put her in school with our son. It was a privilege for my children to safely attend school in person. And then, in September, the world opened up to me again. I suddenly found I had so much time to focus on the business and was excited to get back into it! I realized I had to pivot because forty percent of my pre-pandemic business had been in-person home visits with parents of babies less than one year of age. Clearly, those were off the table for a while.

I'd refused to be a victim of my circumstances and changed my life outlook during the pandemic to focus on the things that I could influence, such as movement and mental health, lowering my expectations of my children and myself and granting myself grace. We'd come out the other side, and now it was time to give energy back to the business and redefine my offerings.

I had started an online membership portal in March, literally one week after the pandemic had shut the schools down. Though the launch wasn't what I hoped it would be with the early fear of the pandemic, I started to infuse my effort into its resurgence. I'd lost my precious home visits, which I loved so much due to the connection with parents, versions of my former self—not to mention getting to hold and cuddle precious babies, who are pure joy and innocence. I missed those! However, I found a new joy connecting in my online group with mothers of different backgrounds across the world. The connection was there; I just had to look in a different place for it.

However, I still needed more to replace the lost forty percent. I had created a Helping Moms Sleep class as a bonus for my online Helping Babies Sleep School. All of a sudden, this class took on urgency and a need to be rejuvenated and shared to help other moms who were burning the candle at both ends and who might not have the privilege to slow down as I had. I also realized that people in this time don't just need another online class; they need human connection and accountability, and so I turned it into an online live six-week coaching program for tired moms to sleep efficiently and wake up feeling rested. I was able to use my clinical training as a chiropractor to build the content and my newfound love of morning rituals, which never would have exploded without the pandemic.

This pandemic happened *for* me rather than to me. I'm taking better care of myself. I'm proud of the decisions we've made for the kids and for my business. I can see all the ways I have pivoted in my life and business to be creative, do what feels right for our family, and focus on happiness. It's not always perfect. There are definitely bad days, but the overall feeling is that this has been another lesson in life.

Don't be a victim of your circumstances. There are always things you can do to change the outcome or the outlook. Less is more. Surrender to the simplicity in life. We often make things more complicated than they need to be. Sometimes it takes pulling away all the busy, all the noise, to sit in the quiet, hear the lesson and learn to trust your instincts.

About Dr. Sarah Mitchell

Dr. Sarah Mitchell is a chiropractor by training but found her passion empowering parents to teach their little ones to sleep and parent confidently night and day. She's a bestselling author, a thought leader in the baby sleep space, and a sought-after sleep consultant in Silicon Valley. Her book, *The Helping Babies Sleep Method — The Art and Science of Teaching Your Baby to Sleep*, is an Amazon bestseller and one of the top-ranking books in pediatrics.

After having kids, she found it hard to regain the energy she had before kids and dove into the science and behavioral patterns related to waking well rested. She noticed that this was a common complaint among the moms she works with. Their babies are sleeping through the night, but moms are still tired. Seeing the need to help moms like herself, Helping Moms Sleep Coaching was born.

She helps tired moms sleep better and wake up energized, giving them more patience for their family and focus for their work. She's a proud member of the Behavioral Society of Sleep Medicine and currently contributing to research on maternal anxiety and sleep teaching. She wants you to know that you can have **great** sleep and happily wake up before the kids.

www.helpingbabiessleep.com | drsarah@helpingbabiessleep.com | IG: @helpingbabiessleep

CHAPTER 11

The Juggle Is Real

by Steph Woods

"The key to juggling is to know that some of the balls you have in the air are made of plastic and some are made of glass."

– NORA ROBERTS

I was in a classic scroll hole on my phone when a tweet caught my eye. During a Q&A session, someone had asked author Nora Roberts how she balances writing and kids. She said the key to juggling is to know that some of the balls you have in the air are made of plastic and some are made of glass.

If you drop a plastic ball, it bounces with no harm done. If you drop a glass ball, it shatters. You have to know which balls are glass and which are plastic and prioritize catching the glass ones.

We have built a life in which we are so busy focusing on juggling that everything seems like it's glass—and the most important thing ever. This one little nugget of knowledge has changed just about everything in my business and my personal life during the pandemic.

Before the pandemic, I was becoming an expert juggler (or thought I was). On top of running my own business, I was supporting courses at the Stanford Graduate School of Business, designing engaging content so that the students could absorb the most information. I had worked with a variety of faculty, from professors at the cutting edge of their fields to lecturers brought to Stanford because of their mastery of a subject, and even a handful of A-list celebrities, such as Tyra Banks and Alex Rodriguez.

Those were the classes I enjoyed working on the most. I was invigorated by giving someone without an academic background the confidence that what they had to share was valuable at such a high level and that they could teach it effectively.

I remember a huge realization about my purpose in life when, moments before her very first class began, Tyra turned to me with a look of panic and excitement and said "I am so glad you're here! I couldn't have done this without you!" At that moment, it dawned on me how fulfilling it felt to help her share everything she had learned in years of building her business empire. It was empowering, and I was hooked.

That moment was the catalyst for me to start my own business that would bring what I do to a whole different world, the world of online entrepreneurs. From my experiences at one of the top business schools in the world, I can bring the same confidence to small business owners and entrepreneurs, help them grow their businesses and ultimately help them increase their impact. Talk about purpose!

◆

I am extremely lucky to be part of a university that acted so quickly when COVID-19 invaded. Over just one weekend, my department, the Teaching and Learning Hub, was tasked with setting up each and every course in progress to be taught online, something that was historically frowned upon at Stanford, which values in-person learning. We created virtual teaching best practices and a recommendations document for instructors.

By Thursday of that week, we had a plan for a virtual spring quarter as well. One email from the dean, and we sprang into action like a fast-acting drug. We moved our workspaces home, stocked up on toilet paper and hand sanitizer, and upgraded our internet plans.

And so began our next chapter, professionally and personally. We were hurriedly pushed into our new reality almost overnight. I felt like a baby bird, shoved from the nest and clumsily flapping around. Little did we know that great things would come out of being forced to learn to fly.

◆

The reality of this "new normal" was hard. Emotionally and mentally, I could just handle less than before the pandemic. In learning design, one of the main pillars is the idea of cognitive load. Your brain can only process so much at one time, and when you receive more information than it can handle comfortably, it leads to frustration and compromised decisions.

As an instructional designer, I design courses in a way that makes it easier for students to understand the material, and more of it sinks in. I do everything I can to give them shortcuts to make connections, little tricks like metaphors, examples, and the way I structure the class, all to reduce the effort it takes for my students to understand what we're teaching them. It's a lot like the energy your body needs from the food you eat. Your brain only has so many "calories" to expend before it needs to be replenished and rest.

With the pandemic consuming us, we have fewer brain calories to work with, and so what few we have become extremely precious! I had to learn how to prioritize, and I had to do it quickly. It became obvious that I would have to decide which balls in the air were glass and which were plastic.

Before, I was so busy searching for all the answers and fulfillment outside myself, and when I could no longer do that, I started to find that the answers were really within me. I started to trust myself and my vision for my business more. After all, the pandemic was the perfect time for entrepreneurs to invest in creating digital courses.

Kids home from school, lowered brain calories, and all-new stressors meant less time to spend working on projects and with clients, and without that, their income would come to a screeching halt. It became more and more clear that time was exactly what these entrepreneurs needed and that a course was the answer. Creating a digital course can change your business to rely less on your time while leveraging your genius to impact countless others! This was a huge opportunity for me to help shape businesses that could survive a pandemic!

It felt I had (forcefully) been gifted this time to reset, to reprioritize my purpose, and shape my business to help so many others. Mentally, there was a shift too. I became more confident in my purpose in this incredibly uncertain time. Isolating myself in quarantine to stop the spread of the virus also removed a lot of social distractions. Time once filled with happy hours, dinners with friends, and weekend brunches was now available for working on my business.

Time is a tricky thing. It's something that we really have so little of, yet sometimes we take it for granted. We see time as a luxury. We create this image of wealthy people being so lucky they don't have to fill their days with work. The luxury here is the choice of how to spend your time.

Many entrepreneurs work tons of hours so that they can make it and then choose for themselves. We work hard now because someday it will be worth it, and that makes us feel super guilty taking that time away from sitting behind our computers to do anything else, even if it's spending time with our own families.

What a lot of entrepreneurs don't think about is how to create a business model that takes the same amount of time to help 100 clients as you would spend helping two clients. That's where online courses come in.

Since courses are a product you can create once yet sell over and over, they are the perfect thing to add to your business when you want to work less but make the same (or more!). When you focus on creating a course that you can leverage, you are able to scale your impact and income without taking up any more of your time that is so precious.

◆

Since becoming so clear on my purpose in the last few months, I've made it my mission to help entrepreneurs create businesses that efficiently leverage their time, part of which comes from my experience with my own family. Since before I was born, my dad has run his own business. (I like to think that's where I get my entrepreneurial spirit!) He owns a trucking company. His business was a huge pull on his time, and as a result, a huge part of our lives.

As fun as it was to run around the pallets in his warehouse on weekends, the business was always there, even when it was inconvenient. On one family trip to Disneyland, Goofy saw him on his huge 1990s brick of a phone and came over and teasingly played with the antenna while dad tried to solve a problem one of his drivers had hundreds of miles away.

I love my dad, and I love how much his business has done for us, but I just wish he didn't have to be on call. I am so thankful that we got to go to Disneyland, but I'll never forget how crappy it was, as a nine-year-old, to have to put all the magic on hold so dad could take a work call. My dad worked around the clock to give his clients the kind of service that made him proud, but there is another way to run a business—a way in which you need not sacrifice the quality you're giving to your clients and students but still don't have to give them all your time!

In learning design, everything that doesn't move your student closer to the learning goal is a distraction. It's a kind of essentialism that isn't too different from what Marie Kondo preaches. An organized home and a successful course have two common elements: simplicity and intention.

Marie observes, "The real problem is that we have far more than we need or want." So many courses suffer from a bloat of unrelated ideas that leave the students confused, underwhelmed, and unmotivated. Many course creators stumble upon this honestly, wanting to give their students every bit of information that might help them, but it does way more harm than good. When clients are having a hard time deciding whether something should be part of their course, I challenge them to think of what would happen if they didn't include it. Would their student fail to reach the goal?

We have to be intentional about what we give to our students, about what is essential and what is not. In education, "sparking joy" means sparking connections in your students' minds and ultimately leads to creating ideas, insights, and action. In essence, a course is a promise for a transformation. You are giving students the steps to go faster from where they are to where they want to be.

In a way, creating a course is giving your students back all the time that they would otherwise spend learning on their own. They're getting a huge shortcut, learning from your years of experience. I've seen over and over how my course opens options for my students. Maybe they want to reach more people and expand their impact, take on fewer clients, or get out of the one-to-one business model altogether. A course gives them that choice. The luxury of choosing how to spend your time.

Every day, I get to help my students and clients launch courses on everything from "how to convert leads to clients in DM conversations on Instagram" to "how to create a routine that nourishes your skin and increases your confidence." I watch them create courses out of things they usually do with clients (like a "basic makeup application for busy moms") or things they have learned on their journey of creating a successful business (like "how to increase retention rates at your salon by making clients feel more like friends"). No matter what the topic is, figuring out the combination of what your audience needs (and will pay for) and what you're naturally good at (and lights you up) creates a sweet spot to create a course.

By shifting the focus from a one-to-one model to a one-to-many model, you're no longer spending your hours working with clients but instead empowering them to do as much as they can with your guidance and then jumping in to give them a little nudge in the right direction when they need it.

◆

One of my favorite professors to work with at Stanford is the behavioral scientist and author Jennifer Aaker. Dr. Aaker is an expert on how meaning and purpose shape our choices, and she digs into this in her class "Rethinking Purpose." Her students are challenged to rethink happiness, aim for purpose, and gain insight into how to infuse a feeling of purpose into organizations they will lead. In a way, this pandemic has challenged me to rethink purpose in my life and business, just as Dr. Aaker's class does.

As a child, whenever I complained about how hard something was, my mom responded with four simple words: "No pressure, no diamond." It was always annoyingly true when I was younger, a kinder way to say, "Suck it up!" but has recently become a mantra of mine. In forcing me to prioritize the balls I juggled, the pandemic was the pressure to take a step back and gain clarity on what my purpose is.

Before, I felt like a jack of all trades. I was good at a lot of different things, but there was no clear path to what my true purpose was or how to feel fulfilled. With the newfound pressure, it started becoming more and more clear.

My mother, a teacher, has instilled in me the importance of education and how good it feels to support others on their path to discovery. My father has instilled in me that it *is* possible to run a successful business but also challenged me to find a way that was less dependent on the hours you put in. My background in the academic world, my need to empower others, other past experiences, jobs, and interests (that had previously felt a little all over the place) fell into alignment for the first time.

Now, my mission is clear: to help entrepreneurs create businesses that efficiently leverage their time (and give them the luxury of choice). I now do that by helping them launch successful online courses.

◆

I propose the same challenge to you: Take a step back and think about what feeds your soul, what is essential in your life, and where you want to put your time and effort. Challenge yourself to determine which balls are glass and which are plastic—which will bounce and which will shatter. Which are truly essential? Ask, "What would happen if I don't do this?"

Then take action. Plan your days around the glass, and delegate or eliminate the plastic.

What can you stop doing in your business? Can you hire a social media manager and stop worrying whether your audience is getting enough engaging posts? Stop doing your bookkeeping and tax prep? How about creating an automated system for the things you do over and over? Hire an online business manager who helps keep projects and deadlines organized, so you can spend your time on the tasks that only you can do? (Psst, I did that, and it's *wonderful*!)

What about in your personal life? Hire someone to clean your house for you? Maybe order those groceries to be delivered? Instead of cooking, order DoorDash for dinner a little more often? The possibilities are endless.

The truth is, not everything you're doing right now needs to be done by you, and when you really figure out what is and what isn't, you will gain the luxury of choosing how you spend your time.

◆

This is the beauty of creating online courses. Once you record what you teach your clients, it becomes the lessons and modules within your course. You're automating the things you do over and over when working with clients, and then you can impact many more people than you had time to before. Record it once, and people can watch it over and over. It takes the same amount of time to teach one student as it does to teach 100 students. You're outsourcing your teaching time to a recording of yourself, so you can spend your time focusing on what actually needs your attention after the basic understanding is already there.

◆

The pandemic has had both its challenges and its gifts. For one moment in time, we're all forced to pause. We're forced to give the highest priority to what's truly important—our health. We're forced to spend time with our loved ones instead of hours in traffic. Each of us is forced to think outside the box and find new ways to connect, forced to step into new roles that we usually don't have—and that brings about growth.

Although dealing with uncertainty is always a struggle, I smile to think that for a lot of kids around the globe, this will be remembered as the time they got to stay home from school, and moms and dads were there too. We just were present with each other.

If that's not a silver lining, I don't know what is.

About Steph Woods

Steph Woods is a learning designer and course creation expert who specializes in value-focused educational experiences. She has worked with a variety of clients, from professors at the top-ranked business school in the world to A-list celebrities, such as Tyra Banks and Alex Rodriguez.

Working as an instructional designer at Stanford, she has mastered learning design techniques that she now brings to business owners, educators, and entrepreneurs. She is passionate about creating methods for simplifying life and business through creating profitable digital courses and utilizing online marketing strategies to sell with ease.

When she's not working with entrepreneurs or at Stanford, Steph loves being a leader for her local chapter of The Rising Tide Society or hanging out in her hammock with her pug and a good book!

www.stephwoods.co | hello@stephwoods.co | IG: @stephwoods.co

CHAPTER 12

Go With the Flow

by Jenn Cino

"Life can be hard for one of two reasons:
1. Because you're growing.
2. Because you're staying the same."

– UNKNOWN

Have you ever walked into a party full of the popular girls and immediately felt self-conscious and inadequate, completely convincing yourself that you probably have a big piece of spinach in your teeth and look like an idiot?

Yeah, me too—except it kept happening even after high school, figuratively with my business ventures. I spent years in comparison mode, debating if my creativity, knowledge, and business plan could ever compare to *hers* or *hers*. I found myself trying to mimic others' style, content, and ideas, and in the process, I lost what makes my business mine—my crazy creative brain, my risk-taking personality, and my voice.

I let the opinions of others dictate my idea of success. I told myself that I needed to invest tens of thousands of dollars into people who sold me a pipe dream that I would be just as successful as them. I had anxiety over finances, over the future, and over my worth. I daydreamed about having a business that wasn't mine. A business I hadn't worked for or deserved. A business that was built upon someone else's accolades. Nothing productive ever came of me trying to compare myself and measure up to other people who I had deemed "successful." Sure, it was inspiring at times, but it wasn't mine. I had been inspired to the point of silence and self-doubt.

But one day, I woke up. I woke up from this dream of this imaginary box that I had stuck myself in, this box that whispered to me that I had to stand out *but not too much*; I had to speak my truth *but not too loud*; and I had to be an entrepreneur *but not like that*. There is no doubt in my mind that there were other people who had convinced me I wasn't good enough, but I gave them their power by allowing that to define my path. There were people who told me that my way wouldn't work, that my ideas were too risky, and that the only way to succeed was to be *just like them*... and for a long time, I believed them.

I woke up, but I didn't wake up to a thriving bank account and customers banging down my door. No, I woke up to a government mandate ordering me to close down my gym—my brick-and-mortar business that I poured my creativity, time, energy, love, passion, and money into. I was shocked.

But I woke up.

From that very day back in March of 2020, I woke up to the realization that I had an out. I no longer had to behave this way or that way, take shit from customers and clients who didn't appreciate me or my passion at all, and I didn't have to keep pouring time and money into a business that would keep me stuck for as long as it owned me.

I got to work. I always knew I had burning potential inside of me, that I could build a successful online business. I just had been so focused on proving it to the world that I lost my spark in the midst of it. I dug deep. I wanted to be respected like I respect experts in my field, but how could I do that without being an expert? How could I step into unknown territories and surround myself with people who were years (and millions) ahead of me? How could I have a viable business when I was good at a lot of things but not great at one thing?

Well, I did what the experts do. I became great. First, I gave myself permission to become great, and even if I didn't quite believe it yet myself, I surrounded myself around people who believed in my greatness.

So how do *you* become great? You dig deep, and you find something that has profoundly impacted you and your life. You reverse engineer all of the situations and experiences around that *thing,* and you teach others how to not make the mistakes you did. That's all business is, right? Take your expertise, education, and experience, and help others through that process without the trenches and ditches you had to cross. You give back to the world in a way that you wish the world had given to you.

I'll take you back to the day that I began to figure it out. Spoiler alert: I wasn't *actually* an expert (yet), but I had the experience behind it to propel me in the right direction.

I remember driving down a long country road with nothing but me, my thoughts, and a good friend on the other end of the phone. I was thinking out loud to her, explaining my passions and ideas and all those things that light me up (with a good side of *"Oh shit, what am I going to do now?!"*). And then it hit us.

"Why don't you teach women how to exercise around their menstrual cycle?"

It all made sense—except it didn't. Sure, I get my period. I know how to exercise. But how do I combine the two? An answer I didn't have at that second, but an answer that I was determined to find out. I got to work. I researched, read books, looked up scientific papers, and borrowed beliefs from a few friends. I signed up for a course to become a specialist in the field, because as serendipity would have it, I had the prerequisite qualifications needed for this *exact specialty*.

I taught myself how to be an expert. Even when the science confused me, I remembered how it felt to be put on hormonal birth control at age fourteen for period problems, and that pushed me forward. I remembered the painful six years that followed my own hormone journey and how I wished I'd had someone who had talked about this. I thought about the millions of women who are going through what I went through and how badly they need me right now. *I taught myself how to be an expert...* and now I'm going to teach you.

1. Find your niche.

    If you try to speak to everyone, you end up speaking to no one. Unsure what your target market or niche should be? Think back to a point in your life—a struggle, a triumph, a pain point—and ask yourself if the knowledge you learned through that process can be applied to someone else to help them. If the answer is yes, you may have found your niche. Your niche is important to clarify because without personal experience or passion behind it, you won't have much to hold onto when times get tough (because they will, pinky promise).

2. Research the heck out of it.

    What is your ideal client struggling with, and what information will change their life? Once you have researched the steps and combined them with your personal experience, make a plan on how you can implement this information into a program, course, or masterclass. It doesn't have to look perfect; it just has to work.

3. Talk to your people.

You can't make money if your doors aren't open. You need to sell the hell out of what you're selling, and you need to do it every day. Walmart doesn't just decide they're going to take a day off and close up shop. They're open every day. Their ideal clients know this and know they can rely on them to be open when they need it most. I'm not saying you need to work all day every day. But it is 2020, and there's an app for that.

4. Expect the best; expect the worst.

Your road to becoming an expert will be a rough one, filled with ups, downs, parties you don't get invited to, parties where you walk around with spinach in your teeth, and parties you feel like you don't deserve to attend. Show up anyway. I can say with full confidence that all of the struggles and road bumps on my journey have taught me incredible lessons, even if those lessons cost me thousands and thousands of dollars. Make mistakes, bless them, release them, and grow bigger and stronger from them. Oh, and then write those mistakes on a piece of paper and throw that shit in a fire!

If there's one thing I've learned on this journey over the last year, it's that opportunities come when you get back to being you. If you spend your days dreaming of being someone else or having someone else's business, you deny the world the opportunity to receive the gifts you have to share. Can you imagine if someone had the information you needed at a trying time of your life and they decided they weren't going to share? Don't be that person. The world needs you, your expertise, and everything that makes you you. It's time to wake up. The world is waiting.

About Jenn Cino

Jenn Cino is a Certified Hormone Specialist, personal trainer, and the creator of fit. period., a women's wellness brand dedicated to educating women on hormone and cycle health and supporting transformations from the inside out.

After years in the industry and hearing non-stop damaging rhetoric around dieting, nutrition, and health from other personal trainers and wellness professionals, she knew the industry needed reform in a powerful way. Jenn went through her own journey of imbalanced hormones and health issues after coming off of birth control and knew there was more to women's health than what we are taught or told.

In addition to writing for Forbes as a hormone specialist, her expertise has been featured in publications including Byrdie and Sunday Riley, and she's been interviewed on numerous top-ranked podcasts. Jenn is passionate about teaching women about how their menstrual cycles can be their superpower, how your body needs *more* nutrients, not less, and how women can achieve all of their goals by working with their hormones and not against them, so they will never have to restrict, shame, or diet again.

www.fit-period.com | hello@jenncino.com | IG: @lifeasjenn

CHAPTER 13

Whoever You Are, Be It

by Hayleye Edwards

"It takes courage to be yourself in a world where you are constantly told that who you are isn't enough. Being yourself is the biggest gift you can offer yourself and others. Be brave enough to show up who you are without an apology."

– ASH ALVES

Have you ever read a motivational quote or a book about someone's life or success and thought, "That could *never* be me. I could *never* do that."?

Well, girl, that was me in March of 2020, the month the world shut down. I'm a twenty-something mama of two, a toddler and a newborn. I've worked in numerous different job genres and had three successful but *very* different careers that I loved. Two of them were ripped out from under me, which broke my heart but ultimately led me here to the *best* place I have ever been, and it is just getting better.

It is so crazy how life can be so normal one day, and then *boom*, something happens that turns it all upside down. For me, the upside-down point was the pandemic hitting in March 2020. In a day, the world changed for so many, including me. Every day I wondered if my job was safe and if my family was going to be okay. We had just moved to a new city, and I'd just found out I was pregnant. My husband's job as a first responder was day by day, and the only certainty was uncertainty. Like so many, I was thrown into living through something I never thought I'd experience, something that caused me to pivot and create something I never knew I wanted or needed.

I am so thankful life happened the way it did because it was the catalyst to becoming a woman I never knew I could be. In fact, I *never* wanted to be this woman, but I *love* her, and she is who I want to be forever.

I am here to tell you that you may not be doing what you love or want. You may not even know what you want. Or you may have found that what you thought you wanted has shifted. That's okay. I've been there. I didn't know what I wanted for myself, not what I truly wanted until I was forced into a position where I had to pivot or fail hard—not the kind of fail that is easy to come back from, the failure that can leave someone full of self-doubt, depression and a level of financial strain that feels impossible to bounce back from.

It has been a long journey to finding this woman. I have been working since I was fifteen, starting in a small surf shop in the back garage hanging bikinis and singing at the top of my lungs while doing it. I loved it. I loved working and having something to show for it. That's never changed.

Along the way, I have had so many ventures. I loved essential oils and making soaps, so I started a business selling my creations at farmers' markets. I had a handmade children's clothing business. I loved making the clothes and was selling them out but was left feeling stressed and unfulfilled. I worked as a teacher and loved teaching little minds, but I loved the little mind I created more. I have taken blood pressure, worked filling out medical questionnaires, waited tables, made coffee, worked at a registration office, and many more in the pursuit of finding what I loved. I was always looking for a way to make money and feel in control of my life. Even when things would drastically fall apart in other areas of my life, work was a constant.

Ten years from that back room hanging up swimsuits, I have a pre-med degree and an education degree. My family thought I was destined to be a doctor, but I had other ideas. I thought I'd found my calling as a medical assistant at a hospital until the hospital went bankrupt and laid us all off. It was my first experience with having something I loved ripped out from under me.

Then, I went into teaching, another profession I loved, but I had my first baby and quickly found that I loved being with my daughter more than being in a room teaching other people's children. That led me to look for a work-from-home position, where I could be a mom and work at the same time. I began working remotely for a multi-billion-dollar company building relationships with customers for the company. I was excellent at my job, and it gave me a purpose I didn't know I needed. I dedicated so much of myself to this job. I sacrificed time with my daughter and the newborn memories for this job, going back to work only two short weeks after having her. I was working hard toward a promotion and being a corporate boss in this job. I wanted to go up that ladder.

Then March 22, 2020, happened. The world was turned over by a world-wide pandemic. Our company had so many meetings and so many calls of reassurance telling us that we were fine! I felt such relief that the company had made it through! Or so I thought.

Just a week after receiving an email saying we were back up to pre-COVID speed, I logged into work to an email saying I was laid off—not just me, but all California workers. I was devastated. How did we make it through the toughest part of the pandemic and then just all get laid off? I felt defeated. Like every job I ever loved that gave me purpose, this one got ripped out from underneath me. I was broken, and I felt like a failure. I needed this. I needed this job to be a better mom and wife and to help take the financial burden off my husband. Well, after a few days of sulking and tears, I went job hunting.

I remember looking for jobs alongside millions of people. There was nothing, nothing in the three fields I'd worked in and no jobs where I could still semi-raise my daughter at the level I wanted to. I saw an ad for a telemarketer for a credit card company. I thought, "Well, this is it. I am going back to work for minimum wage and will do a job that people despise getting calls from because that's what I have to do." That was my rock bottom.

It wasn't even about the job. I am a firm believer that you do what you have to do for your family, and no job is too small, especially until something better comes along. It was my rock bottom because I never knew I could feel so defeated, so unsuccessful. I felt like a burden to my husband and like a failure to him and my daughter. I was always losing these jobs I thought I'd be in forever. It was a small consolation that it was through no fault of my own. It was always due to layoffs or the pay being too small. I sat at my kitchen counter filling out COVID tracing and telemarketing applications in a depressed state, just praying for a break. I searched for the silver lining that had to be somewhere, hiding.

Then one day, my sister-in-law called and asked if I ever thought of going back onto social media, and this time, working in it—doing what I did in the corporate world of customer service, just on a trendier and fast-growing platform. To that, I gave a hard no. I had no desire to get back onto Instagram, personally or professionally. I always despised social media for myself. I see the extreme value as a business, but for me personally, I never wanted to get back on after cutting ties originally.

She ended up convincing me and giving me a chance to help her with her social media management business to see if I liked it. I was doing a lot of admin work that really helped me learn what I wanted to do. I am forever grateful for her seeing me at my worst and giving me the chance to do better and be better.

This is where my new journey began. I was at such a low point that I jumped into doing something I loved on a platform I couldn't stand. Thank God I did. I spent a month with my sis figuring out what I wanted, then a month building clients, and then months after that working harder than I have ever worked in my life to create something out of nothing. I mean, I really had never been so tired and mentally frazzled. I loved it, though! I look back now, and I see that I learned so much in those few short months.

I undervalued myself, I was wearing too many hats, I had to nail down my perfect clientele over and over, and I wanted to quit at least a dozen times. It wasn't because it wasn't something I loved but because I felt like I was such a small fish in such a huge pond. Who would want me? Yet every low-priced client was such a *big* deal. It was a chance to prove to myself and my family that I could do this. I set goals, I hit them, and then a client would off-board or fall off. It was something I had to learn very quickly. There were always changes in this business, but it didn't mean I was failing. It didn't mean history was repeating itself. I was creating my own history. Little victories were actually huge ones, and the small losses were ones I needed to account for and plan for.

One day, I got introduced to a mutual friend who offered me a spot in her coaching program, a program that was life changing. Not only did I learn so much, but the program also showed me just how much I am worth, just how much knowledge I have, how worthy of success I am, and how hard work was going to take me where I didn't even know I could go.

In three and a half months, I quadrupled my income from the company I was working for before. I am building a successful social media engagement business that has turned into a small agency while being an involved mama to a two-year-old and a newborn. And it was all because a pandemic swooped in and took away the job I thought I'd be at forever—all because I hit a low I never knew I'd hit because I was forced to pivot and, thankfully, decided to jump into something completely unknown when the opportunity arose. It didn't happen because I ever wanted this. I didn't want it because I didn't know it was possible. It is all because I made the decision to pivot.

It didn't really hit me that being an entrepreneur and working on social media was my calling until I was working one day, and a quote came up that said, "I am finally the woman that I always knew I could be." I remember reading this and thinking, "I never ever dreamed I would or could be where I am. I never knew what I was capable of, and I never knew I could succeed." It was then I realized something I will never forget.

I'm becoming the woman of my dreams, and she is everything I never knew I could be, but how I love this woman, and she is who I want to be forever!

I have learned so much from the pandemic hitting, but the biggest thing I learned was what I am capable of, what I can accomplish, and as cliche as it sounds, that nothing is impossible. Whatever you choose to do, whatever your dream is, it may be the hardest thing you have ever done. It may mean so many long nights going to bed way too late and getting up way too early. It may take every single bone in your body to keep going, but you can do it. You can get there if you want it or need it bad enough.

Maybe you are working three jobs and barely scraping by. Maybe you are in a field that is making you depressed and causing you an emptiness, or maybe you just want more. Whatever stage of life you are in right now, there has to be something you'd love to do every day. So what is it?

It is okay to be unhappy in the situation of life you are in, but you aren't going to get where you want by waiting for the perfect opportunity to come along. If the pandemic hadn't hit, I wouldn't be here. I took advantage of a terrible time, and I pivoted because I had to.

Maybe you are in the same position where you are forced with a decision: pivot or stay stagnant, stay comfortable but unfulfilled. Maybe you have a dream, but you think it's insane. Maybe your dream is one you think you'd never make money at. Or maybe, just maybe, you are so content with life and what you're doing that none of this applies to you at all. That's okay.

I am here to tell you it is okay to not know what you want or to be in a place in your life feeling unfulfilled. You may be right out of college feeling awful that you spent four or more long years working toward something you have outgrown or have no desire to do. You may be fifty-five and working a job you have been in for twenty unhappy years. You may still be living in your childhood room at your parents' house, completely unsure of what you want to get out of this life. That's okay!

Wherever you are right, now you can still pivot. You can still find what you love and work like hell to get it. Your starting point is to write down every single thing that makes your heart happy. Write down what you would like to do day in and day out and then rank them. Then create a plan. Take a step to a better you and a better life. Be the woman you never knew you could be but that you love! I'm here cheering you on!

About Hayleye Edwards

Hayleye Edwards is a mom of two, wife, and high-touch social media lead generation and DM nurture strategist who empowers busy female entrepreneurs to release the hassle of social media lead generation and nurturing to natural sales. She finds, nurtures, and through natural selling, converts leads into buyers and clients with her authentic, personalized, and proven SCOPE method.

Hayleye has a Bachelor of Science in Science and worked as a teacher prior to finding her passion as a client engagement strategist at a multi-billion-dollar publicly traded company. In 2020, the Hayleye Edwards Co. was founded with the primary focus of building long-lasting relation-ships and increasing prospect-to-client conversion using her authentic, human-targeted lead generation method. Her methods have resulted in clients doubling and tripling their sales and client base in two months or less.

Her expertise has been featured in Authority Magazine, Medium Magazine, and other publications. She's passionate about relieving the stress of lead generation and organic social media engagement off busy female entrepreneurs, empowering them to enjoy the parts of their business they love while still giving their clients the love they deserve.

www.hayleyeedwardsco.com| info@hayleyeedwardsco.com |
IG: @hayleyeedwardsco

CHAPTER 14

A Series Of Bold Moves

by Dr. Nikoleta Brankov

"You don't have to figure out your life's purpose right now...You've got to figure out your next bold move."

– UNKNOWN

Are you continually struggling with self-doubt and remaining persistent in your goals? Is fear holding you back?

Maybe you want to start a podcast, write a book, or pivot in your career, but the fear of failure is too crippling. You're concerned about what other people may think of you if you miss the mark, so you figure it's better not to try at all.

Fear can keep us from pursuing our dreams, but it doesn't have to.

I've always loved learning and putting it into action, something that has served me well in becoming a doctor. In 2017, at the beginning of my dermatology residency, I immersed myself into entrepreneurship by reading books, attending webinars, and learning from a digital marketing agency. I was on a constant search to improve myself, learn new things, and grow outside of my medical career.

In 2019, I was in the middle of my second year of a dermatology residency and had just been accepted for a fellowship in dermatopathology. My husband and I just completed a sixty-day health challenge where we had increased energy, reduced fatigue, and lost weight. At the start of 2019, I was in the best shape of my life and reached a goal weight that I was prior to medical school. I felt incredible.

I joined my first mastermind that year, where I met the most incredible human beings who all pushed each other in their lives and business goals. Being a part of a group of women that were all goal-oriented and supportive is a different world than what I've been exposed to in medicine. I formed friendships that I still have to this day. I set a goal to launch a New and Noteworthy podcast, and I accomplished it. I was doing all of this while also being pregnant, due in August of 2019!

Preparing to become a mother, I did everything humanly possible to dig deep into my birth journey. I had hired a doula, which I had never heard of before a friend used one for her birth, and took an eight-week birth class. Preparing and educating myself in the birth process was exciting for me. I changed providers to a practice that has physicians and midwives, hoping I could have an unmedicated birth with a midwife.

I listened to audiobooks, watched movies such as *The Business of Being Born*, and researched the differences between birth in the United States versus Europe. When I was in medical school, the OB-GYN rotation was not my favorite; however, it all changed for me when I was pregnant. I became so immersed and interested in everything.

In 2019, I traveled to California and Ohio to see my family for baby showers. It was an incredible year, having my first baby while starting my chief year in dermatology residency, excelling in my podcast, and continuing to learn more.

I had such high hopes for continuing that momentum into 2020 until the world ground to a halt. As the world came screeching to a halt in March, so did my ideas and plans. Being in the medical field, the pandemic took so much energy from me. Watching my colleagues going out on the front lines and putting their life at risk without having enough personal protective equipment was very painful. Dermatology in-office appointments were moved to online appointments, and we had to figure out a way to adapt quickly and efficiently. I put business ideas and plans for 2020 on the back burner, taking a pause in my business and podcast while finishing my last year of dermatology residency in the middle of a global pandemic.

I'd learned how to be open to support and how to redefine my goals before, but the pandemic was when I actually integrated and applied these lessons into my life, beliefs, and existence.

In the past, there were times I had uncertainty, and I called upon them and the lessons they taught me to navigate the new normal of 2020.

The Power of Basketball and What It Taught Me

I was born in 1990 and raised in Cleveland, Ohio, by parents who were Eastern European immigrants from the former Yugoslavia. My mom's family immigrated when she was fourteen years old, and my dad came when he was in his early twenties. Coming from an immigrant family, hard work was a way of life. I didn't complain, I appreciated the value of working hard, and honestly, I was just so thankful for the opportunities in this country.

Despite not knowing much English, my dad built a very successful dental technician business. My parents taught me about the "immigrant hustle"—there are no excuses for not working hard, and this attitude conditioned me for all the adversity I would later face in life.

When I was ten years old (back in 2000), I fell in love with the sport of basketball. I used to watch Kobe Bryant and was obsessed with the Lakers. I became focused on becoming an excellent basketball player, and I would study and analyze all the top NBA player's techniques. It was a dream of mine that I would one day play in the WNBA. I loved the thrill of a challenge.

As a seventh grader, I took a chance and tried out for the middle school basketball team. I still remember the day the coach posted the final roster list of accepted players for the seventh-grade team. I didn't see my name on the list. I checked again and again, but it wasn't there.

I was devastated. I knew that I could be great if they just gave me a chance. But the coach doubted my abilities, and he didn't think I had the drive to do well. So instead, I decided to try out for track that spring. I was stellar at running the one mile, and I always finished with excellent times. Meanwhile, I took private shooting lessons for basketball and worked for hours and hours on perfecting my game. My past failure only motivated me to keep working harder.

For eighth grade, I moved to a top school in northeast Ohio. I tried out for the basketball team, and this time I made it. We had a fantastic season, and I was even more motivated to keep improving my skills in preparation for high school.

One year later, I made the varsity team as a freshman, a *huge* accomplishment. I love that quote from Michael Jordan: "I've failed over and over and over again in my life. And that is why I succeed, and I can accept failure. Everyone fails at something, but I can't accept not trying."

Basketball taught me about teamwork, discipline, work ethic, and how to always strive toward improvement. Greatness was a part of me. But then, my world came crashing down when my coach decided to cut me from the varsity team after playing for two years.

I couldn't believe it. I worked harder than anyone else. Everyone at school was shocked. At that moment, I started to rethink why I even played. Did I play because I loved the game? Or for some other reason? I was reminded that I played the sport because it was fun and I loved the competition. And that even though I got cut, I somehow knew that all of this happened for a reason.

From Starting an Accelerated Medical School Program to Setbacks with the MCAT

After being cut from the varsity team, I used the setback to redirect my focus into my studies. I took advanced placement and honors classes. I graduated high school in the top six percent in my large class of 500 students, and I had a GPA above 4.0.

As a senior, I was accepted into a six-year BS/MD program, which basically means you can become a physician in six years by finishing your undergraduate Bachelor of Science degree in just two years. This meant that I could be a doctor when I was twenty-four years old.

I now had a new mission. I started college only one month after graduating from high school. And let me tell you—this was like no other normal college experience. It was intense. I only came in with about four credit hours that I was able to use for Spanish. But other than that, it was a ton of work.

In my first semester, I completed twelve hours. In the fall semester, I completed twenty-three. For the next semester, I completed twenty-five, and for the following summer, I completed twenty-two. So basically, within one year, I had senior college-level status based on my credit hours. I excelled in my studies and received all As. Only one more year to go until I would be in medical school.

On the flip side, I had no time to learn about other things in life that would make me a good doctor, like nutrition and self-care. I was solely consumed with my studies.

The time came to take the MCAT, which is the pre-entrance exam for medical school. The MCAT is one of the hardest pre-entrance exams for graduate school, and I had to achieve a minimum requirement on this exam in order to start medical school at the ripe age of twenty.

I took the test and scored below the cutoff by *one* point. I studied some more, took the test for a second time, and again missed the cutoff by *one* point. It defeated my confidence. I no longer felt worthy of the profession, and my self-doubt crippled me. In my eyes, this setback was defining my worth.

I wasn't able to start medical school along with my other friends in the accelerated BS/MD program. Two years went by, and I felt so left behind. I started to doubt if a medical career was really meant for me. But like the setbacks I had experienced in the past, this one would propel me toward greatness.

During my third year of college, I took a light load of classes, twelve credits per semester, played more sports, and gave myself permission to pause and have more fun. I began to read about plant-based lifestyles, nutrition, and preventive medicine to help me become a better doctor in the future. I also drew closer to God and began to rely more on my faith and His plan for my life.

During this time, I met my now-husband, Eddy, who played a big part in my spiritual walk. I started to let go and give up control by letting God lead my life. I took an extra year off to process all this and prepared to take the MCAT again—hopefully, for the last time. I took the test and scored very high, and I was accepted into Loma Linda University School of Medicine in southern California.

I still started medical school after four years—it was just a very non-traditional four years. When I did not score the best on the MCAT in the past, I remember thinking it was such a setback, but it was actually a huge blessing. The time allowed me to refocus my life on things that mattered, like my faith and relationship with my now-husband. Once I had finally been accepted, I cried tears of joy. God had answered my prayers and freed me from my self-doubt and feeling of unworthiness.

Pursuing Dermatology in Medical School and Redefining Success

I moved to California and started medical school at age twenty-two. It wasn't easy being apart from my family, but I was so excited about this new adventure. I had decided to pursue dermatology, and I wanted to ask mentors for advice on what I could do to have the best experience. I remember asking a medical student for some tips, and this is what he said to me:

"How do you think you will get into dermatology without any physicians in your family?"

Dermatology is one of the most competitive fields in medicine, and what he was saying was that I shouldn't even try. He mocked the fact I was even pursuing it as an option.

I decided not to listen to him. I knew what I was capable of. I sought out mentors in dermatology early on, and I published several papers throughout medical school. I understood that networking was essential to get me where I wanted to be.

Fast forward to my fourth year of medical school. I married my sweet husband, and the time had come for me to match into my specialty! But another setback hit me hard: I did not match into dermatology. This hurt. I cried again. But deep down, I knew that all my other experiences had led me to this point, and I couldn't give up. It didn't matter that I'd experienced yet another setback. It didn't matter if other people didn't believe in me. Nothing else mattered but my belief in myself.

I worked day after day on research projects and publishing. I worked insanely hard. And then, during the following year as an intern, I matched into dermatology. If I had listened to all the doubters who told me to face the music and take a different path, I wouldn't be here today doing what I absolutely love.

But even though I had achieved my goal, I still had some growing to do. In the struggle to match into dermatology, I had lost myself a little bit. I gained twenty pounds, and I was no longer active. I was pessimistic, and I complained 24/7. My money mindset was horrible, and I didn't take the time to do the things that I enjoyed.

What is the point of success if you lose your health, your faith, or don't take care of yourself? As a doctor, my job is to help others, so how can I do that effectively if I don't know how to help myself first? It was then that I decided to make a change.

During my first year of residency, I took my health and life seriously. I got into reading about personal development and started taking on healthy habits to succeed physically, emotionally, and spiritually. By surrounding myself with this information and people with similar values, I required new skills and a stronger mindset. If I came across someone negative, I didn't let them enter my life. I created healthy boundaries while also stepping out of my comfort zone to become the best version of myself. Throughout this time, I kept my focus on God and His plans for me.

In hindsight, my experience during my third year of college, of not starting medical school with my friends at the age of twenty, gave me the realization that I had to surrender and let go of the rigid plans I made for my life. After those two years of undergrad, where I finished my bachelor's degree, during my third year, I gave myself permission to focus on other things. I did a lot of reading and decided to go vegetarian and lead a more plant-based life. That year, I scored very well on the exam, and during my fourth year of college, since I had already finished my degree, I worked for six months at Cleveland Clinic as a dermatology researcher and was accepted to Loma Linda University School of Medicine. This year, I gave myself permission to pause and traveled for a few months to Spain and Serbia. I started medical school in California that summer refreshed and ready.

Remember, each setback I faced in my journey led to another, which resulted in more and more growth. To become confident, you have to be willing to try, even in the midst of failure. You have to have faith in yourself and take action, despite what others may think.

Failure is supposed to teach you, not define your worth. Even without the pandemic, the first half of 2020 was a challenging year. I knew that in the first six months of 2020, I had to be preparing and studying for my dermatology boards in July, moving across the country for fellowship, finding new childcare, transitioning jobs for both my husband and me, all while finishing my dermatology residency. And all this in my first year of motherhood, nursing, and exclusively pumping around the clock.

All our dermatology conferences and board review were canceled in March through June, and in June, with little more than a month's notice, we found out that our dermatology board certification exam was moved from July to October. By June, I had already done four hours of studying per day, often totaling thirty hours per week on top of work and being a parent, and I was on track to finish my boards-prep studying schedule. However, since the exam was moved, I now had to repeat all these hours of studying again in the fall prior to my exam.

While it was initially upsetting, I didn't have the luxury of time or energy to stay upset. And in the end, it was a gift to have the exam moved to a later date because my furniture wouldn't even have arrived. I would have had no place to study and prepare, and it may have been harder to reach my goal of breastfeeding the first year, balancing all of the commitments I had.

This year also looked different because I missed going to church and seeing people who are so important to me. I missed being able to travel to see my family in Ohio when the pandemic hit, and I was wondering when my parents would be able to see their first grandbaby again. Gyms started to shut down in March. I love fitness and love exercising, and the gym was a community for me.

All of the momentum I had created in 2019 with my podcast, brand, and entrepreneur goals were put on hold once the pandemic hit. I gave myself permission to pause. Knowing that finishing residency, studying for boards, moving across the country during a global pandemic, finding new childcare, and adjusting to a new home was going to be new life changes, I had to give myself permission to take a break.

I had to redefine support and asked my husband to help on the weekends and weeknights with childcare so that I could study for my exam after long workdays in fellowship. I had to learn to delegate more, ask my nanny to help cook and clean, and be okay with letting go of control. I did not have any more of me to give, so for me, 2020 allowed flexibility without needing to control the outcome by being open to receiving help and support and redefining my goals.

If you are facing a challenge in your own life, consider these questions:

What could you pause in your life?

What could you let go of?

The answers to these questions will help you achieve your own success.

About Dr. Nikoleta Brankov

Dr. Nikoleta Brankov, MD, is a board-certified dermatologist, top-ranked podcast host, and nationally recognized skin, hair, and nails expert. She teaches women how to identify (and stick to) their customized, perfect skin care routine so they can start loving the skin they're in—*even when makeup-free!*

Dr. Nikoleta has been featured in Forbes Magazines, NBC News, Sunday Edit, and more. She's guested on multiple podcasts and is a frequent speaker at nationally recognized dermatology conferences. She earned her doctorate at Loma Linda University School of Medicine, has published nineteen peer-reviewed articles in dermatology journals, and co-authored two peer-reviewed dermatology book chapters.

She's the founder and creator of the Healthy Skin Blueprint, a step-by-step online program that helps women understand the science behind their skin, which products to use and why, and how to feel completely confident in their own skin. She's worked with more than 10,000 clients and patients in the past decade to help them love the skin they're in.

Dr. Nikoleta resides in Houston, Texas, with her toddler son and husband, who also happens to be a dermatologist. She's passionate about learning and personal growth, movement, plant-based living, and helping women step into their most confident, healthy, and supported versions of themselves.

www.drnikoleta.com | info@drnikoleta.com |
Instagram: @drnikoleta | Podcast: Millennial Doc™ Podcast

CHAPTER 15

Circumstances Don't Define Your Success

By Crystal Duan

*"If you change the way you look at things,
the things you look at change."*

– WAYNE DYER

It might be a little unconventional to admit this, but I actually profited during the pandemic more than I did before. I'm not a six-figure business owner, though; I'm a newbie.

I started my business during the pandemic after procrastinating on it for *months*. I was maxing out my credit card to pay rent in Los Angeles before and wondering if I'd make it through March. Then everything closed, and suddenly, people needed what I had to offer.

I'm not Amazon. I'm not Zoom. My product isn't even tangible. The most basic description of what I do is I'm a *spiritual consultant*, and the best way to sum up the services I offer people are tarot readings and life coaching.

It was my first time investing in any coach. Before the summer ended, I'd shelled out $10,000 in business development help. And I didn't go into debt; I actually went full time in my business by month three.

This was a time for me to unravel my ideas of what was conventional and what wasn't. It's just as egoic to be overly confident as it is to be under-confident, and boy can I tell you—the ideas of what I needed to start my business *completely* changed because of the pandemic and the results I was getting.

Most people would say not to start a business *during* a pandemic, but I didn't listen to that. I had been learning to follow my intuition since I was a young child, and my life experiences, even at the young age of twenty-five, had validated that over and over again.

A little about me: I went to school at the Missouri School of Journalism, the top public university for journalism and strategic communication. I graduated in 2017 with a degree in investigative reporting. I was setting myself up for a life of writing for newspapers. I even got published in big publications such as the Washington Post and Bustle.com and interned for the most prestigious regional dailies such as the Indianapolis Star and the Minneapolis Star-Tribune. I had it made as a journalist—but I wasn't living the avant-garde style I really wanted.

I got really into the intersection of psychology, spirituality, and social justice when I was in college. The Ferguson shooting death of Michael Brown and Black Lives Matter protests occurred in 2014, an hour from my college campus. One year later, the resulting racial tensions throughout the state were amplified when students came head to head with the administration protesting their response to various incidents on campus. As a journalist, I was tasked with providing objectivity when covering both sides. But I was so curious as to how people seemed to live in different realities.

As a result, I began studying up on tarot, astrology, and the spiritual origins of the Myers-Briggs Type Indicator in the writings of its original theorist, Carl Jung. I learned about energy, mused on the misunderstandings and psychic differences of people, and found a way to incorporate my knowledge into every ounce of reporting I did.

Most people wouldn't expect a political journalist who has covered two elections to pivot so heavily into doing spiritual work full time. But I saw no dissonance when I decided to leave the full-time reporting world in 2019, less than two years into it professionally. At the time, I told myself I would make it as a big spiritual teacher and also get into writing the theories I'd come up with in the last five years.

Instead, I did a good job procrastinating. Before the pandemic, I was vending tarot readings at markets in Los Angeles but had not really worked on making it a real business quite yet. By day, I'd work as a virtual assistant for two separate companies, and on the weekends and during evenings, I'd set up my plastic table and crystals and open for business.

People would step up for twenty-dollar readings. I'd look up their birth chart and use my Tetris-like knowledge of the cards to piece together the story of what I saw. I'd make $300 a day to work five or six hours. But it wasn't something I took *that* seriously. I'd learned the craft of reading to serve people, and I didn't know how to make bigger bucks. The biggest gigs I'd work were celebrity parties where I'd get paid a flat rate, but I'd never taken one-on-one private clients.

When the pandemic hit, I had no more gigs to work. I didn't immediately panic when things shut down in March because I was already working from home. Now everyone else was *also* at home, and I had nowhere to distract myself during the day.

So I decided to take my business model virtual and make it donation-based. I posted in some Facebook groups that I was doing pay-what-you-can readings over Zoom video calls. I figured, Why not give people some existential comfort right now? I'd been doing that since I was twenty, so what did I have to lose when nothing else could be controlled?

Within three weeks, I'd made $1,500 in donation-based readings reading for thirty clients. People were blown away at the insight I gave them and were tipping me sometimes hundreds of dollars. If they didn't pay me that much, they were telling their friends. I left my Calendly open for a month while contemplating what I was seeing. How was it that I was having my best business month yet and even had a couple of new coaching clients willing to pay $100 per hour per session?

I recalled a few Instagram Lives I'd watched featuring successful entrepreneurs. Many had touted the power of relationship marketing and how the real money isn't in selling yourself but in building connections with others.

I'd always been extraordinarily good at this. I could make friends with virtually anyone I met, whether it was at the grocery store or a party or in line for an event. I was always able to accept the need to just be myself.

And now I was believing in that. That first $1,500 I made *with no expectation* was the spark it took for me to see it for myself: The power *is* in people, and a pandemic doesn't weaken that. It strengthens it. It also showed me that if people chose to pay me $150 by choice, I have something they needed. And where there is need, there is a market.

So I started going to free networking events and befriended some business coaches. I invested in my first mastermind without any idea how I'd pay the first $1,000 but trusting in the relationship I had already built with that coach. Using her advice and the emotional support I got from the group, I started advertising larger packages and custom-tailoring my sage intuitive insight to what I sensed the entrepreneurial community needed. I didn't define myself as a tarot reader—I used tarot, MBTI, and astrology to complement everything I did. I attributed my knowledge and expertise to it, but really, I tried to embody that these tools were a part of a *lifestyle*, not just something I was secondary to.

Really, the pandemic helped me step fully into my own personality. My takeaways are that I should always listen to what *my* truth is, that truth was found in the insane ability I have to charm people and make them feel seen, and that they will put their faith in me because I first put my faith in them without expectation.

Getting into messy action really gave me clarity around this. I was prepared and committed to whatever the outcome of hiring that coach was, and also confident that we could talk through it if I couldn't manage to pay her. And my faith took flight and helped me land every paying month with ease and grace.

But because I made almost $2,000 in my first month of the pandemic from donation-based tarot reading and then went full time in my business *before* learning to scale it, I finally realized I had proof of concept that I have value.

This solidified to me that I should *not* listen to what other people thought made sense. I'm still learning this right now as my coaches advise me to take everything, even their own wisdom, with a grain of salt.

Growing up and after college, I never felt like I belonged in any world I set foot in. My career is tied to wanting to overcome that, and I thought

I had to belong to be successful, chasing different career ideas and procrastinating on my full-time dream to be recognized for my insight.

But in a time that people call unprecedented, where success and stability have been redefined, I finally was able to fit in. I am different, and my truth as to why I am proud of that is also valued. All I had to do was pay attention—and also experiment with no expectation until I got the evidence back.

But that was really about me learning to accept and embrace my own gifts and to receive value for my real worth, not the limited worth I had set my value at.

About Crystal Duan

Crystal Duan is a spiritual strategist, consultant, and tarotist currently based in Los Angeles. Her business and life consultations combine tarot, astrology, MBTI, and other spiritual typing systems with helping clients with the language to transform their fears into abundance and creativity. She specializes in unblocking emotional resistance and translating your blocks into manifestations.

A former journalist, Crystal's work has also been featured in the Washington Post, Bustle, and the Minneapolis Star-Tribune, among other publications.

Niche statement: I help clients new to spirituality and personality type embrace their unique gifts and cultivate their unique route to manifesting through esoteric tools such as tarot, astrology, and MBTI.

www.crystal-duan.com | crystal@crystal-duan.com | IG: @crystalxduan

CHAPTER 16

Your Plan Will Guide You

by Andrea Woroch

When I think back to my childhood and what I wanted to be when I grew up, a money expert was far from those dreams. This was definitely not a role I ever intended for myself, nor one that I even thought possible. In fact, there was a period of time in my twenties when I was anything *but* good at managing money. Money went out faster than it came in, and though I was enjoying life on the outside, I was suffocating behind closed doors. As the mountain of bills kept growing, I got buried deeper under debt until it felt like there was no way to climb out.

However, sometimes it takes getting to the bottom to realize your way out. At that time, I decided enough was enough, and I had to take charge of my life if I wanted to change it. I did the things I tell people to do nowadays as a financial expert and writer if they want to get out of debt. Such steps include setting a budget, tracking expenses, working side gigs, cutting up credit cards, paying with cash, getting a roommate, eating at home, curbing impulse purchases, saving for emergencies, stop keeping up with the Joneses, and so on.

Slowly but surely, I began making progress and dug myself out of debt. The load of bills that once crushed me felt lighter, and I could breathe again. From there, I found myself writing about my own journey and helping others by sharing my own experience. I discovered a passion for guiding others out of their own murky financial situations and realized a whole new world of opportunity through my own personal money struggles.

Of all the advice I offer these days, perhaps the most valuable tip that I always go back to no matter what is the importance of being prepared. Preparation is the key to safeguarding both your personal and financial life, and it can be achieved by saving for emergencies. An emergency savings is there for you to lean on in tough times and protects you during short-term financial storms. It gives you breathing room when times are tough so you don't have to divert from the life you worked so hard to create. It gives you peace of mind. It ensures your family is taking care of no matter what. This is something many of us needed more recently than ever before, but what I learned in the past year is that being prepared for the unexpected doesn't stop at building a healthy savings account. There are so many other areas in our personal and professional lives where learning how to prepare our mind for unexpected circumstances and being ready to pivot at any given time is ultimately the key to survival. Being adaptable and flexible in life plans can make or break you, and it's what sets many of us apart.

As the pandemic took hold of our health and our country, my entire world flipped upside down. That's when panic set in, and questions began to explode in my mind: How would I continue my work if TV stations no longer allowed in-studio guests, something I based a large portion of my business on? Or how would I continue coaching other experts to build their brands and prepare for media appearances if such opportunities didn't exist? Beyond the professional stress, there were the personal issues at hand, too, like childcare. Pre-school abruptly shut down, and babysitters were nearly impossible to find, making it hard to work with my two young girls at home, who constantly bombarded me with their non-stop needs.

With so much at stake with my business and my family, I realized I couldn't waste a minute reeling in self-pity or doubt. I was staring down two different paths—one of uncertainty and one of action—and it dawned on me that everything I experienced those ten or so years earlier, when I decided debt wasn't part of my destiny, was actually making a full circle back to guide me through this difficult time. You see, taking charge of my finances then allowed me to change the course of my future. It is this that gave me the confidence to know that I am fully in control of my life in every situation, even when it doesn't seem possible. How I proceeded from that moment on was going to change the outcome the pandemic had on my professional and personal life, and I surely wasn't going to let it destroy all the progress I made over the last decade.

Instead of allowing the universe to dictate my outcomes and wallow in worry, I realized in that moment that focusing on all the things that were out of my control was a waste of energy. Instead, I decided to overlook the what-ifs and double down on what was right in front of me the whole time. So I focused on the things I could control and made a plan for how to manipulate the situation at hand.

Knowing TV stations would still need guests to fill their shows, I moved quickly to create an at-home set with superior lighting and sound and began emailing my contacts immediately to offer remote interviews that touched on timely topics, showcasing my studio-quality home set. Setting up a dedicated space for these video calls and remote TV interviews made it easy for me to participate in last-minute requests without having to rearrange my living room or kitchen to accommodate urgent media needs. I also didn't have to worry so much about the constant mess that became my reality, thanks to my children, who were stuck at home all day.

Understanding that the pandemic posed serious financial hurdles for many individuals and families, I began writing feverishly to develop a series of timely media tip sheets that focused on the financial struggles many consumers were already experiencing or may potentially face in the near future as a result of business closures and job loss. This included advice on how to manage bills and other money matters during uncertain times, how to prepare for emergencies to safeguard your family's finances, and more.

I pitched these topics to new and existing media contacts and received an overwhelming response, booking dozens of shows on the topic over the first few weeks that the stay-at-home order was implemented. More interestingly, I realized that hosting remote TV interviews opened even more doors as I was able to join shows across the country that would have otherwise been a challenge pre-pandemic. This allowed me to expand my reach, and I worked to develop new contacts in cities I may not have thought to reach out to in the past.

Beyond managing my own on-air appearances, I also found an opportunity with media coaching, launching a new course to help experts and professionals prep for remote TV spots as well as help fine-tune their presentation skills, which included things as basic as setting up a camera shot and adjusting the lighting for everyday virtual calls. I realized a lot of people were not accustomed to virtual video, and some expert guidance was needed to boost confidence and ease the shift toward this new normal.

Although our world is far from back to normal, I have settled into this new way of working and living, focusing on the positives that have come out of it. For instance, less time traveling for media spots means more time to spend with the people who matter most or doing things that bring me happiness. All those hours I spent driving or flying can now be spent playing with my girls, cooking homemade meals, or enjoying the outdoors.

Not to mention all the money I have saved on travel has been a great benefit to our household budget. I'm spending less on airfare, hotels, meals away from, and childcare, which means I have more money to put toward other goals, and I even enjoy a splurge like a dinner out with my husband without the added stress of how that will impact our finances. Ultimately, I've slowed down a bit and am enjoying the ease of life that has come with that.

As I share my experience over the last year and my ability to focus on what I could control instead of wasting time, energy, and stress worrying about all the things that were out of my control, it's important to understand that this was possible thanks to the financial safety net I created for my family. You see, building an emergency fund, as I mentioned earlier, gave me the confidence that I could try something new without fear that it would impact my ability to pay bills. Part of this financial safety net also included a budget backup plan in which I knew exactly which expenses I would cut first to accommodate a change in income. With that, creating multiple streams of income has also given me stability and confidence in knowing I can lean on one income source in the event another dries up. In the end, it's all about having a backup plan for various situations since you never know what lies ahead.

Here's what I learned: At any given moment, our lives can change course, and that can be an unsettling feeling. In these moments, however, regardless of how out of control you may feel, it's important to realize just how much power you actually have over the direction your life goes. The way you respond to any situation, good or bad, and the actions you take shortly after will shape your future outcomes. Still, it's not just what you do in response to a situation but what you do in advance that can have the greatest impact on your circumstances.

Preparing for the unexpected may seem like a conundrum of sorts. After all, how can you make preparations when you don't know exactly what you are preparing for or why? However, there is a lot you can do to control the unknown, even when it is completely uncertain what that unknown is. In fact, this is what I have based my entire business around. Planning for unexpected financial emergencies is not exactly easy to do, but it is possible and essential.

When establishing an emergency fund, there are a couple of rules to follow.

First, take a full audit of your finances to figure out just how much you spend in any given month. Since there are both fixed and fluctuating expenses, you can take the average of those non-fixed costs to determine a monthly amount. Once you know just how much you spend per month, you can set off to save for that rainy-day fund. Your ultimate goal should be to save around three to six months of living expenses set aside in a separate fund, but more if you're self-employed. This may seem like a lot at first, but be mindful of unnecessary costs that you may be able to cut when times get tough to accommodate a lower budget.

To boost this savings quickly, consider cutting a few nonessential items for a few months and put the money you save from those costs directly into this savings account. I also find that automating money directly from your checking account or paycheck each month right to savings takes the work and effort out of it. Not to mention, when it's out of sight, it's out of mind, and you won't even miss these dollars when you become used to living without them. You can even go so far as setting up separate emergency funds for various expenses that can come up, such as a car maintenance fund, pet health bills, or home repairs. You can never be too prepared.

Another essential element of preparing for the unexpected that cannot be overlooked is the importance of creating multiple income streams. When you have money coming in from different sources, you gain a layer of financial protection. This ensures you have another income source to lean on in the event you lose your job or your hours or wages are dramatically reduced.

When it comes to diversifying your income, a lot of people get stuck in figuring out what that could look like. However, there are a variety of opportunities out there, whether that includes leveraging your professional skills for freelance opportunities or turning a hobby into a side hustle. You can even find odd jobs around your town or right from your home computer that can help you earn extra income on the side. For instance, websites such as FlexJobs, Upwork, and Fancy Hands feature freelance gigs, from marketing to public relations to content writing. Meanwhile, Remote.co posts remote jobs with both full-time and part-time gigs.

Even if you find it difficult to come across a side hustle that leverages your skill set, there are many other things you can do even without experience. You can get paid to conduct online research, tutor high school students, help with posting on social media, offer virtual assistance to small business owners, or even something as basic as pet sitting. Being open to the possibilities out there is the first step.

Although setting up an emergency fund and diversifying your income are two important steps toward safeguarding your finances and lifestyle, there's another even more vital component that often goes overlooked, and that is keeping your living expenses low. It's easy to get wrapped up in the excitement of a raise or promotion and start spending more on things like a bigger house, nicer car, and fancier clothing. However, giving in to such constant lifestyle upgrades can make your financial foundation unstable, leaving you little wiggle room in the event of an unexpected bill, job loss, or recession. The lower your living costs, the less stress there will be if your financial situation changes.

So ask yourself this: Is how you're spending your money now serving you, your family, and your ultimate life goals? Do you have enough breathing room in your budget to accommodate a financial blow? If not, it's time to take a step back and really consider what brings you happiness. Then focus more of your energy and finances on those things while cutting back on the rest. Ultimately, this will help make your life feel more fulfilling and potentially give you much more flexibility in your budget for the unexpected.

You can begin assessing your expenses by downloading my free budgeting worksheet on my website at www.andreaworoch.com. And remember, your money shouldn't cause you stress. Instead, look at it as a tool to create the life you've always wanted, which can be done even in times of uncertainty, as long as you use it wisely and plan ahead.

There are a lot of vulnerabilities that come with the unexpected, but there should also be some comfort in knowing you are more in control of your own destiny than may seem possible at the moment, even when life seems to be working against you.

Our lives are shaped by the choices we make and how we decide to respond to new opportunities and obstacles. Sometimes these pivotal life moments are self-inflicted, while other times, they are forced upon us.

In either circumstance, though, being prepared and knowing your ultimate life goal can help steer you in the right direction so you can proceed with confidence. Just remember that your budget is an aid that can guide you through those tough times. And those who prepare ahead and protect their finances can find more strength through any obstacle. This will give you the confidence and ability to be flexible when things don't go as planned so you can pivot with ease and stay on course to achieving your dreams.

About Andrea Woroch

Andrea Woroch is a nationally recognized money-saving expert who has helped millions of Americans find simple ways to spend less and save more without sacrificing their lifestyles. She is specifically passionate about helping women take control of their financial futures so they can stress less about money and spend more time and energy on the things that matter most, like their families and businesses.

Andrea has appeared on hundreds of TV shows across the country, including *Today*, *Good Morning America*, *Dr. Oz*, *CNN America's Newsroom*, and *Inside Edition*. In print and online, her stories and advice have been featured in *The New York Times*, *Money*, *Forbes*, *Cosmopolitan*, *Redbook*, *Time*, *Huffington Post*, and many more. Andrea is also a regular writer for a variety of personal finance and lifestyle sites, including US News and World Report, and she is a member of the Smart Money Squad at GoBankingRates.com.

www.andreaworoch.com | andrea@andreaworoch.com | FB/TW/IG: @AndreaWoroch

CHAPTER 17

The Value of Joy

by Abbie Mirata

*"I keep my ideals because in spite of everything,
I still believe that people are really good at heart."*

– ANNE FRANK

I have carried these words with me since I was young. Anytime I'm faced with challenges or people who harbor ill will, I come back to these words and her story. She was faced with her own pandemic, one of hate, and she had her own version of quarantine hiding in that attic, leaving the world much too soon in the concentration camp. But her ability to keep joy, her ability to look past poor behavior to the human behind it, her optimism through all of it gave her the best life possible for the short one she had.

My husband and I made a decision to open a brick-and-mortar business. We had what one would perceive as a pretty awesome life. Our kids are grown and out of the house, we are still very young, we have flexible high paying jobs, we travel and enjoy life. So why on earth would we want to dive into the most difficult, time-consuming, and unpredictable world of owning a restaurant and all that entails?

We put a lot of thought into this and were ready to create something. We wanted to build culture and community right where we lived, to create a place for friends and family to gather, talk, and celebrate. We had a special attachment ourselves to Jeremiah's Italian Ice, as the brand's base is in our hometown. Not only did we celebrate there, but our family had tough conversations over that Italian Ice. That's where my ex-husband and I told our kids that they would be joining me to move across the country and far away from him and their friends and family. I needed to create that space in our new home. I was also drawn to working with young people, giving them a safe space to grow and learn, and doing my part to create better adults for our future.

For almost twenty years, I operated within the walls of the corporate world. It wasn't horrible, but it wasn't blissful either. When I finally made the decision to leave, it was more about the fact that I didn't feel valued than I didn't like my job. I didn't feel like people really liked me. Perhaps I made a difference to the company's bottom line, but not to the hearts and minds of the people I worked for and with. This was my perception and therefore my reality. It was an interesting revelation the moment I gave my notice. The most beautiful notes and calls came out of nowhere. I remember thinking to myself, "Where the fudgesicle have you people been all these years?"

So I pivoted into owning my own business—from one version of crazy right into another! With all the knowledge, all the preparation, all the investment, and all the excitement, we were ready! And just as we were ready to open up, the world shut down. While most folks were scrambling to figure out how to change, we were struggling with how to start. We couldn't do any of the things we had planned—no grand opening, no big push to get tons of people through our door, reduced capacity rules, additional costs in cleaning supplies, and no events to cater. Should we even open? Yeah—we should. Now more than ever, people needed that place. Now more than ever, our staff needed a safe place. Now more than ever, we needed to create a community in whatever way we could.

In my corporate career, I employed over 300 salespeople, ran a multi-million-dollar budget, implemented million-dollar projects, and I've never felt as appreciated and needed as I do scooping Italian ice and handing it to my customer. Throughout this pandemic, we have been constantly thanked for simply being there. Our customer base is still small but loyal. We've had people who come in because of seeing a coupon but refuse to use it because they are so concerned with helping a small business. Parents needed a break from being cooped up in the house all day with homeschooling and knew that our place was somewhere they could slip away for a few hours.

And then there's my Frog Squad: the most incredible group of young adults I'm blessed to be working with. In six short months, I have adopted all of them. I have watched them create customer service skills and work through employee challenges. They care so much about the success of our business, but more importantly, John and me. Through account-ability, coaching each other, learning our customers' stories, and taking care of all our equipment, we teach them leadership, gratitude, and responsibility.

It amazes me to see them truly understand their impact through all this. I don't know that they would have learned this lesson at this point in their lives without it. We had a meeting about how their actions outside of work can have a huge impact on all of us. If one person were to get COVID-19, they could shut down our entire business and put everyone out of a job for weeks. It was cool to see the light bulb switch on and watch the ones who decided that this space was more important than hanging out with friends or going to the club.

I had started my journey to joy long before we all found ourselves in pandemic mode, but I think thriving through this year allowed me to really understand what I was trying to accomplish. I was finally able to put it into words. I had to live it every day, and I could figure out how to help others find their path. I've also begun to study and have an appreciation for human nature. I find myself constantly questioning it: Why isn't it human nature to put gratitude, empathy, and respect first?

Don't believe me? Ask yourself this question: What is my first reaction when someone cuts me off on the highway? If you were honest, it was most likely something like flipping them off, calling them a name, or getting frustrated. Asking ourselves if they're okay, if they just got a horrible call, or if they're distracted by tragedy are typically not the first things to pop in our minds. And when we do experience something aggravating like this, we tend to hold on to it and project it on others.

In other words, we internalize gratitude and happiness, yet we externalize frustration and annoyance. We keep our happy thoughts to ourselves, and we project our negativity onto others. When we've had a bad day, everyone we interact with from then on out is going to know because they can see and feel it in us. We become moody, short-tempered, and impatient with people who honestly have nothing to do with whatever the original cause of our annoyance was.

This was also a part of me that I wanted to change. I needed to move away from this behavior. I wanted my human nature to default to empathy, gratitude, and compassion. This sounds great, right? We all want that, but none of us seems to be able to figure it out. I realized it's because of two main issues. First, we are looking at it all wrong, and second, it's not a priority.

I know, I know—back up and take that scowl off your face. Let me explain why I believe joy is not truly a priority for most of us. First, we are looking at it all wrong. Most people look at joy as a feeling or emotion. We say things like we want to *be joyful*, *find joy*, or *spread joy*. But you see, feelings and emotions are dependent on our circumstances. When our circumstances are good, we feel good; when they are bad, we feel that too.

Ninety-eight percent of the time, our circumstances are not within our control. If you want joy to be an integral part of who you are, take the emotion out of it. It's time to have a different relationship with joy. I see joy as a value. Our values are the things that guide our actions in any given situation, and we usually don't even have to think about it. There is a process to creating joy as a value, and it begins with making it a choice, then a habit, then a part of who you are. That leads to number two: why it's not a priority.

Thinking of joy this way, making it a habit, like any other habit, takes work, dedication, and compromise. I've seen people accomplish great things with great discipline, yet when it comes to truly making a mindset shift and changing our inner workings, we just don't seem to put it at the top of the list. Plus, a lot of the time, we just don't know how to do it.

I was one of those people. I went on retreats, listened to podcasts, watched TED talks, and read the books, and in that moment, I was inspired. I just couldn't keep it up. I still fell back into normal patterns, saw negativity in others, and projected my biases and feelings on those around me.

One thing I was really great at, however, was following a process. I looked at all my other habits and values. To adopt them, first I had to learn the skill, then I had to be repetitive and disciplined, and then I had to make it non-negotiable. Then, one day, it was just there. It's automatic, like making your bed in the morning, healthy eating habits, going to the gym, or locking your car door when you get out. When you step back and think about it—well, you don't think about it! I realized if I wanted to be better, I needed a process to follow. I needed to understand my end result, and I needed to commit to it like I would anything else.

I started by relating to something I was comfortable with—my workout routine! In particular, what resonated with me about the process I went through to develop a healthy lifestyle and how I could apply those concepts elsewhere and make it easy and fun to build my value of joy! Five exercises to strengthen your Joy Joints™ was born.

And I can tell you, I've never needed stronger ones than in our world today. Between a pandemic and an election year in a cooped-up, divisive nation, I had to call on every cell to operate together to see the best in others, to understand where they come from, and to keep myself in a headspace to move forward, not sideways. Once I realized I needed a new value to guide me and I put a process in place to adopt that value, it became easier and easier, and I became better and better. Strangely, so did everyone else around me. At least, from my perspective—they may not have changed at all, but how I perceived them did.

Strong Joy Joints™ made me a better communicator.

Strong Joy Joints™ gave me more time to do what I love.

Strong Joy Joints™ helped me sleep better.

Strong Joy Joints™ helped me grow my business and serve *all* my customers.

Strong Joy Joints™ opened new doors and opportunities for me.

Strong Joy Joints™ made me a better mom, a better wife, a better me.

With joy as a value, I am in control of my own responses and reactions to the world. I have stopped being a thermometer, reacting to the weather around me, and have become a thermostat, setting and regulating the temperature for myself and others.

With joy as a value, I am able to stop myself from saying or doing things I would later want to take back, from immediately assuming the worst of others, and from reacting out of impulse to a situation without truly understanding the story and the human behind the behavior they are displaying.

Below is the process I had to go through to help me strengthen my Joy Joints™, and I believe these exercises can help others who truly want to do the work to make their own little world a better place.

1. **Cleanse.** Quiet, silence, or remove dramatic and negative content from what you watch and engage with on both television and social media. This could include celebrity drama, late-night shows with political rhetoric or that make fun of people (even people you don't like), negative memes, etc. Be intentional about what content you follow when you are choosing to watch and engage; that makes a difference too!

2. **Stretch.** Stretch to find the good in others. We all have people we don't like, who trigger us, and who push our buttons. People may bully us at work, put us down, or make us feel bad about ourselves. These are the people we tend to complain about, gossip about, and speak ill of. Find something good about them—stretch if you have to. Maybe they are a great dresser! It has to be authentic, or it doesn't work. When engaging with this person, especially if it's a negative engagement, focus on this point. Think about it and even outwardly compliment them on it. Then walk away! You'll feel so much better.

3. **Group workout.** There is nothing more important than finding people to help you along the way and engaging in positive social interaction. One thing we've all learned from this year is how important being together really is and how much we take it for granted! The biggest piece of this exercise, however, is the giving and *receiving* of help. The giving part we've got down; it's the receiving that we aren't that great at. We've been conditioned to believe that asking for help is a sign of weakness when it's the exact opposite! Think about how much you like to help others. Think about how that makes you feel—useful, empowered, and supportive. Why on earth wouldn't you want to give someone else those feelings? Ask for help every single day.

4. **Lift Weights.** This exercise is all about learning to let go. We carry so many little things on our shoulders that we aren't even realizing, and they begin to pile up and get very heavy. When we fill up our capacity with a lot of little things, when a big thing comes along, it knocks us down. This one is hard, but with the foundation of the other exercises already there, you can do it. If someone cuts in front of you in line or maybe says something rude to you in the morning, and by the end of the day, you are still rehashing and reliving it, you've given that person your power. Keep your power. Let it go. You will feel better! Keep your shoulders clear so you can carry the heavy stuff when it comes along!

5. **Balance.** This is about bringing it all together, about understanding the difference between true joy and hopeless optimism, knowing how to help others without using toxic positivity, living out your joy without requiring others to do the same thing, being curious, not judgmental, and forgiveness of others and of yourself.

Each exercise takes time, commitment, and practice. This is meant to be a self-evolution, not a simple mindset change. While I am here to walk you through ways to accomplish all these things, there is one thing you can do on your own to begin the journey. It's very simple. Breathe.

When life happens, take just a few moments. Breathe in and wonder: What don't I know? What story is there behind what just happened? Breathe out and remind yourself how lucky you are to be here, to be okay, to not be in whatever space the person is in that's projecting their inner strife on you. Then, from that headspace, make a choice on how to respond to whatever is going on.

Breathe in empathy. Breathe out gratitude. Choose joy!

About Abbie Mirata

Abbie is a corporate executive, speaker, joy coach, and business owner. From the title of wife and mom to the title of franchise owner to the title of corporate leader, whatever hat Abbie is wearing, she is focused on impacting people, creating community, and building a kinder world. She believes people are looking for a human connection in the companies they do business with. Abbie draws from her experiences to help others focus on cultivating joy and finding the light they give from within themselves, each and every day.

Abbie has almost twenty years in sales, marketing, and training. She has done almost every role from sales to divisional VP to corporate training and operational development. Abbie uses her process of 5 Exercises to Strengthen Your Joy Joints™ to empower individuals at work or at home to be able to gain control of their own responses and reactions to the world, redefine joy as a value, and help you maintain your sanity while keeping your humanity.

www.abbiemirata.com | abbie@livekyndly.com | IG: @abbiemirata

CHAPTER 18

Your Superpower

by Jessica Bird Hagestedt

"We have created a society that honors the servant
& has forgotten the gift."

– ALBERT EINSTEIN

A fifth-grade parent-teacher conference set the trajectory of my early life.

Christine and Mark Bonney sat across a desk from Mr. Christiansen. Concerned looks plastered on their faces, the love and worry in the air were palpable. Mr. Christiansen finished his speech on how well their daughter was performing in school and where she needed improvement and looked at the concerned couple.

Christine and Mark glanced at each other before turning to the teacher. They were about to put to words what had been weighing on their minds. They were concerned, as their daughter had not shown an aptitude in any one subject.

This was extremely important to Christine, as her work had defined her life, and as remarkable work as it was, it was not her passion. She dreamed of becoming a doctor and had excelled in the sciences, but life circumstances had her shifting her focus and trailblazing a career as one of the first women in the world of computer software engineering. From working with the government at a young age to being on the creative team for CAD, she has contributed to our world in immense ways but knew she wanted more for her daughter.

"She has not excelled in any one area, so how are we supposed to support her moving forward?" asked Christine.

Mr. Christiansen stared at the parent sitting across from him for a moment before a smile spread across his face. "Of course, she has an area she excels in. She is talented on the playground. She is an athlete."

And thus began the focus of the next twelve years of my life.

From all-star softball double-headers to competitive soccer tournaments and field hockey matches, my parents invested time, money, and a lot of energy into letting me partake in any and all sports I had time for. They knew that a career in sports was unlikely but also understood the values that sports can instill and the ability to earn scholarships to colleges that may otherwise be financially out of reach.

With their support of my love of sports now fully engaged, I started to realize the opportunity I could have if I excelled enough to stand out. But as I worked my ass off to do this, I was also being taught not to.

My peers were teaching me that I was too loud, too much of a flirt, too quirky, and too much in general. Adults were teaching me that I was not to speak until spoken to and that I talked too much. This added to a narrative that was instilled in me in first grade, that I was annoying and unintelligent and that grown-ups are always right. That belief left me questioning my instincts and who I was at the core.

I slowly learned to ignore my intuition and was solely guided by those around me and what they thought I should do and the athlete they thought I should be. I became disconnected from myself. Sports became an emotional outlet to work through the growing feeling of anger and frustration that I didn't understand and couldn't name.

On the field, I left it all. It wasn't just my opponent I was battling, but myself, pouring out the emotions that weren't safe to display anywhere else. I was fueled by something much more powerful than the passion for winning.

As high school ended, my parents' support mixed with my hard work, passion, determination, sweat, blood, and tears paid off. I was recruited by some of the country's top schools, including Ivy League schools I would have never otherwise had the opportunity of applying to. I felt the pressure to choose the right school and finally landed at the University of California at Berkeley.

As I started my first day as a Cal Bear, I admitted my fear to myself and also finally understood that the reason I chose this school was that it was the closest to home. It felt the safest.

I had no idea what I wanted to major in since I never thought about anything outside of sports. Thinking about myself as being more than just an athlete would mean *me* making a decision about who I was. Yet I still was operating from a place of disconnect and distrust.

Surrounded by students who already intimidated me and seemed to know exactly what they wanted to do with their lives, I still felt like the dumb girl in the room. When I declared psychology as my major, the decision felt fake because I didn't know who I was, let alone what I wanted to do.

As I buried myself in my sport and studies, barely leaving time for the coveted college social life, I began to worry more about my major. It soon became apparent to me that psychology, although fascinating, wasn't bringing me joy.

When painful injuries forced me to take the sideline, I was left reeling with my choice of major and was removed from my one outlet for releasing frustration and emotion. So I turned to food as a crutch. I gained more than the Freshman 15, and it wasn't going away. This affected the way I felt and also negatively impacted my athletic performance.

At an end-of-season meeting with my coach, she bluntly told me my performance was lacking, and she said, "Watch what you eat." That was the catalyst of years to come.

I felt lost. To cope with all the discomfort, fear of losing my scholarship and my identity as an athlete, I decided to take control in the one area of life I felt I could: my body.

Spring of my sophomore year, I began to obsessively exercise, started a low-carb diet, and dove into an eating disorder that I had only flirted with in the past. I began obsessing over food, its quality, and its calories.

Within thirteen days, I had lost all of the extra weight I had been carrying, dropped my body fat down to twelve percent, and hadn't even noticed because I was so lost in the routine.

My coaches and teammates took immediate notice and brought it to my attention. At the time, there was not a smooth course of action when handling disorders. Due to my teams' eating disorder history, the assumption that I was anorexic or bulimic was the label they thrust upon me. (My particular eating disorder was also not well known at the time.)

When they cornered me with this, I was shocked, hurt, felt betrayed, unsupported, and misunderstood.

No, I was not anorexic; I ate food, and I ate "good" food, too.

No, I never intentionally purged food a day in my life.

Yes, I am doing what I thought I was supposed to. I am in the best shape so I can perform as the athlete you are "paying" me to be.

My disconnect from the labels and the insistence of them by my coach, school doctors, teammates, and eventually family and mentors left me feeling isolated, shammed, confused, lost, and ever angrier. The isolation felt deep and dark. It wasn't just their lack of understanding of my situation; it was their lack of trust in me—trusting that I was being honest about eating food and not purging it. Trusting that anorexia and bulimia did not align with what I was doing, how I was feeling, or who I was.

I detached from the team emotionally and continued to focus on my game. It was still my only outlet for anger and these new emotions of betrayal. I felt betrayed by those I trusted and even more so by myself.

Still caught in my emotional turmoil and unsure of my major, my junior year forced me to choose a major or be suspended from playing field hockey, my one rock.

I left it to the very last minute. In my game gear, fearful of not being able to play, I sprinted to the American Studies department to declare my major in an interdisciplinary field. Still undecided, this choice gave me the flexibility to *create* my future.

This choice became the first time I pivoted away from others telling me what to do or who to be. In that single act, I laid the foundation for a skill set that I still use to this day.

College continued, and my eating issues worsened as well as my relationship with my coach, teammates, what friends I had, and my family.

At graduation, I walked across the stage with a degree in Human Health and Behavior in the United States. I created this major with a counselor and defended it with a forty-two-page thesis. Although I should have been proud, I still felt lost, alone, and isolated.

What was I going to do?

With a suggestion from my mother, along with my love of exercise, I earned a certification in personal training through ACSM. My first job was at a large gym chain. It was there that I not only met my future husband but also found my passion for working with women.

I had a few male clients, but it was the women who brought my talents to life. I loved helping them learn about their bodies. Building women's strength, showing them their capabilities, and being their support system lit my fire. It had me staying in a profession that didn't feel quite right for years.

Even with the joy I experienced working with my clients, my gut was pulling at me. The instinct that I unlocked the doors to in college was speaking to me. I was destined for more. Personal training did not fully align with who I was meant to be.

Listening to this voice, I embraced the need to feel aligned, tapped back into the skill I had acquired in college, and proceeded to pivot.

For the next seven years, I changed course and continued pivoting as I dabbled in many careers, attempting to feel aligned. From nanny to executive assistant to physical therapist, each career I pursued felt like a little piece of my purpose, but not fully.

I learned that I loved being around children, experiencing their energy and creativity, but I felt more aligned with teaching adults. I learned that I loved organizing, goal setting, and planning (i.e., taking the guesswork out) for others but didn't feel a passion for the industry I was doing it in. I deepened my passion for helping others get stronger, learning about their bodies, and encouraging their understanding of fitness, but I wanted more freedom in how I guided my clients.

Then, in 2015, nine years after graduating college and what felt like a billion career pivots later, my husband and I had our son, Ezra.

The thought of leaving Ez at three months broke my heart, and that's when I realized that maybe this was who I was meant to be, a stay-at-home mom. Hoping this was my last pivot, I slowly walked away from the traditional working world and into full-time mommying.

Even with all the joy that watching my son grow brought, that inkling, that pull from my gut, told me I wasn't quite where I was supposed to be. Knowing that I wanted to remain at home as much as possible, I decided to pivot in a way that scared the absolute shit out of me.

With support from my husband and leaning on his belief in me, I decided to start my own business. I had wanted to do this since becoming a personal trainer. I had just lacked the faith in myself and the courage to pivot so big at that point. After earning a certificate as a Holistic Nutrition Coach, I launched Balanced By Birdie and a year later turned it into an LLC.

With Balanced By Birdie, I was able to combine my passion for serving women with my passion for fitness and health. I began helping women shift their food and fitness mindset through tools I had learned in both my education and personal struggles. I began teaching non-restrictive eating habits and movement to support their bodies, not beat them up.

My business started off rough. I hit technological walls and financial hardships and learned that marketing was a muscle I needed to develop. Learning my voice, embracing my niche, and creating the BIRDIE Method all took time and a hefty financial investment. But that didn't stop me.

My gut, that voice I had learned to ignore, then barely trusted, was now my loud and clear guide. With each pivot, each step closer to becoming aligned, trust in myself and my instincts were given life.

As a women's health business owner, my inner self was home. This is where I am meant to be. This is where I will bring the most impact. This is where I am aligned. A couple of years later, Balanced By Birdie, LLC, is strengthening its wings and ready to soar.

I have expanded from a one-on-one health coaching platform to adding custom fitness programs and memberships, and I'm the owner of a boutique boot camp. In October of 2020, I had my largest month to date and no longer feel the pressure of the financial red line.

I wake up each morning excited for the day, excited to share tools, create deeper connections, guide more women to step into their power and strength, help women find their healthy balance, and reconnect women with their powerful intuition.

I no longer feel alone. I no longer feel misunderstood because I understand myself. I trust me. I no longer question my body or feel the urge to turn to food and exercise to ease my emotional turbulence.

Reflecting on where I started, I am now grateful for all my struggles. Had I not felt so disconnected and alone yet forced to make a choice, I may not have had my awakening. It was an awakening that has given me the ability to continuously pivot until I felt aligned—the ability to stop relying on others and to start trusting myself.

With every pivot, I was taking one step closer to being aligned, moving through my fear, and listening to my gut. I was tapping deeper into my intuition until I became fully connected with her and trusted her.

I didn't let the fear of the unknown stop me from pivoting away from the people, beliefs, and pursuits that didn't serve my purpose. I realized fear and discomfort were often positive signs that I was growing.

The more I shifted and grew, the stronger the connection to my purpose and my passion became. And with that, the more joy-filled life I led.

I realize my story of disconnect is not unique.

As women, we are taught not to trust ourselves. We are taught to let others tell us who we are to be. We are taught to be small, silent, and quietly stand with a smile—a mere ornament, a bystander in a world of men, making the tough decisions around us. We are even pressured by laws that take our rights to choose and listen to our bodies away from us.

But women are not created to be small. Women's intuition and the force behind it is one of our most powerful tools. This tool terrifies those in power, hence women's history and the way you may feel when you look in a mirror naked, or how you may feel in a group of men or even other women. It's the tendency to apologize. It's the pull to be catty, the feeling that other women are competition.

The more we consume others' ideas that we have flaws that need to be fixed, listen to others telling us women are our competition, and put value into the words of those that tell us we are too loud, crazy, big, or annoying, the more disconnected we become from our intuition, our guiding light, our true selves and how we connect with our power and joy.

If our attention is pulled to focus on the outside, we connect less from within.

The more power that is given to others and emphasis put on who they think you are, the less you become yourself.

I look back lovingly at the story of my fifth grade parent-teacher conference, as I appreciate Mr. Christiansen guiding my parents. I appreciate my parents supporting me in what was to become a defining part of my life. I just wish I had known I could be more than just one thing, that I was more than just an athlete, and that I could trust that pull inside of me, guiding me to be more me.

Women, your gut is your superpower. The next time someone tries to make you feel small or pushes you in a direction you do not feel aligned with, connect with your inner self and listen to that powerful, intuitive voice; let it remind you that you are more than capable, you are more than enough—you are *you*, and being your own brand of you is where the magic begins.

About Jessica Bird Hagestedt

Jessica Bird Hagestedt is a functional wellness coach, fitness, and nutrition expert who empowers fed up and frustrated women to be confident, stronger, and leaner by ditching their diets and hamster-wheel workouts and falling in love with food, fitness, and themselves.

With a lifetime love of fitness, Jessica furthered her D1 athletic career with a decade of studies and certifications in personal training and holistic and integrative nutrition. Through her online functional wellness coaching, she's created the BIRDIE Method, a fun, adaptive, and sustainable approach to help free women from confusion and anxiety around their bodies, food, and movement.

In addition to working with hundreds of clients, her expertise has been featured in Authority Magazine and HealthyWay, as well as on numerous podcasts. She lives in Lake Oswego, Oregon, with her hubby, five-year-old wild child, and two puppies.

www.balancedbybirdie.com | Birdie@balancedbybirdie.com |
IG: @Jessica_bird_hagestedt

About the Publisher

Rebecca Cafiero is an International Forbes business and visibility strategist, TEDx Speaker and top ranked podcast host, bestselling author and mother of two. As the Founder + CEO of the Pitch Club - a for women, by women company - she has worked with hundreds of female entrepreneurs to increase their credibility, visibility and profitability in business. Prior to becoming an entrepreneur, she spent 13 years in Corporate America leading sales and marketing teams. She is a frequent speaker on online business strategy, creating credibility + visibility, productivity and personal optimization. She's passionate about helping female entrepreneurs be seen, heard and valued as an expert in their field.

As a sought after media source, Rebecca's tips have been featured in NBC News, ABC News and publications including Forbes, Reader's Digest, Women's Health, US News and World Report and more.

https://www.rebeccacafiero.com/ | rebecca@rebeccacafiero.com | IG @rebeccacafiero

About The Pitch Club

The Pitch Club community was created for driven + heart-centered female entrepreneurs, professionals, and business owners, who want to work for themselves but not by themselves.

We're on a mission to equip women with the tools to increase their visibility and credibility and build a profitable purpose-driven business (and have fun doing it!).

Join the Community!

Follow us on IG: @thepitch.club

Made in the USA
Middletown, DE
19 October 2022